THE CONTEMPLATIVE CHURCH

Joachim and His Adversaries

George H. Tavard

THE CONTEMPLATIVE CHURCH

Joachim and His Adversaries

MARQUETTE UNIVERSITY PRESS

Marquette Studies in Theology
No. 49
Andrew Tallon, Series Editor

www.marquette.edu/mupress/

Library of Congress Cataloging-in-Publication Data

Tavard, George H. (George Henry), 1922-
The contemplative church : Joachim and his adversaries / George H. Tavard.
p. cm. — (Marquette studies in theology ; no. 49)
Includes bibliographical references (p.) and index.
ISBN-13: 978-0-87462-726-8 (pbk. : alk. paper)
ISBN-10: 0-87462-726-5 (pbk. : alk. paper)
1. Joachim, of Fiore, ca. 1132-1202. 2. Joachim, of Fiore, ca. 1132-1202—Adversaries. 3. Bonaventure, Saint, Cardinal, ca. 1217-1274. 4. Thomas, Aquinas, Saint, 1225?-1274. I. Title. II. Marquette studies in theology ; #49.
BX4705.J6T38 2005
230'.2'092—dc22

2005024882

We thank most heartily the International Center for Joachimist Studies for the use of the cover image of Joachim taken from their marvelous web site where many other images and valuable resources for the study of Joachim of Fiore are generously made available to the public.

http://www.centrostudigioachimiti.it/Benvenuti/Benvenutieng.asp

Note from the series editor.

∞The paper used in this publication meets the minimum requirements of the American National Standard for Information Sciences—Permanence of Paper for Printed Library Materials, ANSI Z39.48-1992.

MARQUETTE UNIVERSITY PRESS
MILWAUKEE

The Association of Jesuit University Presses

Table of Contents

Introduction

There have been many studies of Joachim di Fiore (c.1130-1202) over the last thirty years: general presentations of his life, assessments of his works, of his connection with the Cistercians and of his conception of the monastic life in the Order he founded, analyses of his hermeneutical method, apocalyptic views on the Church, investigations of his posthumous relations with the Spiritual Franciscans, reviews of his religious and secular posterity. Founded by him in the second half of the twelfth century, the Order of Fiore flourished in Southern Italy through the thirteenth century, and then began to shrink. What remained of it, notably the abbey of Fiore itself, was absorbed in the Cistercian Order in 1536. It is not as a founder, however, that Joachim has been remembered, but as a theologian who based his peculiar views of the future of the Church on a method of interpretation that he claimed to have received by inspiration. As a prophet the abbot had considerable success in the thirteenth and fourteenth centuries among the Spiritual Franciscans. Most of the spiritualist movements that have agitated Christendom, before, during, and after the Reformation, have shown traces of Joachim's influence.

The prevailing image of the abbot of Fiore carries with it a heavy dose of naïveté. Most prophets in the history of the world have turned out to be false prophets, and Joachim is no exception. Although the discernment of spirits has been practiced in the Church since the days of St. Paul, and it was exemplified and regulated, in patristic times by Cassien, and in the sixteenth century by St. Ignatius of Loyola, it remains singularly ignored in much religious literature, especially at the popular level.

Practically all scholarly studies of Joachim have drawn attention to the ambiguous historical ties that have existed between Joachim as a theologian or exegete and the popes of his time and of the decades that followed his death. I do not know of any study, however, that has concentrated on the vexing question of a Joachimite influence on the papacy. The question, however, is unavoidable. The memory of the abbot was protected by the popes of the thirteenth century, even when his doctrine was severely condemned by the greatest theologians of the period, by a papal Commission, and by a provincial Council, and when the one movement that revered him ended in confusion, shame, and condemnation after bringing chaos among Franciscans. Why were these popes lenient toward the heterodox trends in Joachim's thought, when they did not tolerate the Cathars?

There is no harm in thinking that abbot Joachim was a holy man. But holiness of life cannot justify or condone intellectual errors and distortions of thought. Joachim has in fact has been called "Blessed," and he remains honored as such in several dioceses of Southern Italy. In certain quarters the wish to have him officially beatified or canonized is indeed still alive and well. On March 30, 2002, the archbishop of Cosenza, Giuseppe Agostino, formally introduced the cause of the beatification of the abbot of Fiore in his diocese,—the diocese of Joachim's birth -, and, with a degree of unconscious irony, he entrusted the case to a Franciscan! I fervently hope that such a cause will go nowhere. Fortunately the formal process of beatification and canonisation includes an examination of a person's writings in light of the Church's traditional teachings. The Catholic faithful have always assumed that, even when the existence of a person who has been beatified or canonized is not historically certain, or even can be historically disproved—as is the case with Juan Diego (see Stafford ¨Poole, *Our Lady of Guadalupe. The Origins and Sources of a Mexican National Symbol, 1531-1797*, Tucson: University of Arizona Press, 1995),—the image of the saint can function as a symbol of doctrinal orthodoxy. While it is normal that the magisterial judgment of bishops, including popes, on someone's teachings, should prevail in official documents, one expects such a judgment to be in harmony with the consensus of theologians in good standing. In the case of Joachim, the most important theologians of the thirteenth century, St. Thomas Aquinas and St. Bonaventure, both of them acknowledged doctors of the Church, unequivocally condemned the doctrines that the abbot had gathered from Scripture with his supposedly inspired new method!

If, whatever his biblical erudition, Joachim was not a reliable theologian in regard to the doctrine of the Trinity, he was at least, some will say, a good Christian and a spiritual person. He was in a sense a good Latin Catholic, who professed to submit his writings to the judgment of the bishop of Rome. But does such an attitude make him orthodox, if, firstly, he did not ask for such a jugdment in his lifetime, and, secondly, his speculations, unchecked, opened a surprisingly post-Christian perspective? After God the Father and the Old Testament there has been God the Son, who became flesh and gave us the New Testament. It was Joachim's doctrine that there must soon be God the Spirit, who will bring the Eternal Gospel and will lead the Church from its present clerical status to a perfect monastic status! If the Holy Trinity is indeed eternal, God's relation to the creation, and in particular to humanity, keeps evolving. The Law of the Old Testament was for the imperfect. Christ's precepts were for beginners. Something else, something better and more advanced, is still expected. It will soon come from the Holy Spirit. It could well be this post-Christian perspective that has recently made Joachim so popular that he is featured in several more or less well-informed websites!

Indeed, my further acquaintance with the writings of Joachim has confirmed the judgment I expressed in the introductory chapter of *Christian Spirituality. High Middle Ages and Reformation* (Jill Raitt, ed., New York: Crossroad, 1987, p. 6):

> Whether Joachim was himself a mystic, the recipient of special graces of spiritual insight, would seem to be questionable... Besides whatever personal piety he presumably had, his pictures, like his vision of history, are matters for the head, not for the heart. They may fill and clutter the mind, but they do not nurture it. A new meaning of Scripture may indeed emerge in subsequent experience, meditation, and insight, but it cannot be invented through intellectual cleverness. Joachim was clever.

I do not wish, in this short presentation, to compete with the major studies of Joachim that have been published over the last forty years, or to duplicate what they have said. I am indebted particularly to the works of Bernard McGinn, Marjorie Reeves, and above all my former professor Henri de Lubac. My topic, however, is not Joachim himself, his writings, or his doctrine. Beyond the career and influence of the Calabrian abbot I am interested in the question that is raised by his relations with the papacy, and, reversely, by the popes' extraordinary regard for a man who, however holy he may have been, turned out to be a false prophet who directed theological hope toward a blind alley. While Innocent IV was critical of the abbot in 1219, Honorius III explicitly affirmed his orthodoxy in 1220, and Alexander IV implicitly endorsed the judgment of Honorius in October 1265.

This topic is relevant in priority to the Catholic Church. It throws an unexpected light on the way in which some of the bishops of Rome, in the solicitude for all the Churches that defines their specific ministry, so envisioned the nature of doctrinal orthodoxy that they actually minimized the necessity of fidelity to some traditional teachings. It raises the question of papal responsibility for the bad things that happen to the Church if the magisterium does not properly fulfill its role of doctrinal guidance. This is evidently of interest to the People of God, for it cannot fail to affect their trust in the declarations that are made by the magisterium.

Since the name of the abbot of Fiore is fairly familiar in religious scholarship I will keep the English form of his name, which happens to be also its Latin form, rather than call him Gioacchino, as in his native Italy. Since, however, the Franciscan who interpreted and applied Joachim's thought to the Order of St. Francis is not so well known, I will, at the risk of inconsistency, call him Gherardo rather than Gerald, the name Gerald being already associated with other medieval personages, such as Gerald of Cambria (Geraldus Cambriensis).

Chapter One (**Joachim**) will present abbot Joachim di Fiore and give an outline of his career and of his doctrines and prophecies. Chapter Two (**Gherardo**) will present what conclusions an otherwise obscure Friar minor in Paris inferred from Joachim's works regarding the providential role of St. Francis and the Franciscans. Chapter Three (**The Politics of the Eschaton**) will describe the political and cultural context that gave the perspective opened by Joachim an unexpected importance. Chapter Four (**The Protocol of Anagni**) will study the recommendations made about Joachim and Gherardo by a papal commission, and show that the judgment of the commission concerning Joachim was ignored by pope Alexander IV. Chapter Five (**The Judgment of Thomas Aquinas**) and Six (**The Judgment of Bonaventure**) will show that, both before and after the Protocol and the papal decision, St. Thomas Aquinas and St. Bonaventure severely rejected the characteristic doctrines of Joachim. Chapters Seven (**The Hierarchies**) and Eight (**The Contemplative Church**) will focus on Bonaventure's extensive corrections of Joachim in regard to the nature of the Church and its contemplative dimension. A brief **Epilogue** will formulate relevant conclusions for the Church of the Third Millennium.

Brighton, MA
George H. Tavard

Chapter 1
Joachim

Geographically the crisis originated in the twelfth century in an unexpected location, a monastery in a remote section of the remote Italian province of Calabria. Theologically it grew out of uncertainties in the doctrines of the Trinity and of the eschaton. Theology and geography merged in the speculations of Joachim (c.1135-1202), the founder of a new monastic order, the Fiorensians.

*

The Calabrian abbot was, for better or for worse, one of the truly creative spirits of his time, though at first sight he seems to be simply a holy monk, eager to practice the *lectio divina* enjoined in the Rule of St. Benedict, and hankering after the peace and quiet that are part of the monastic life. He was in search of quiet when, on his return from a pilgrimage to Jerusalem, he entered a Cistercian monastery. After spending some time at the abbey of Casamari in 1183 and 1184, he was elected abbot of an independent community at Corazzo, in 1185 or 1186. He managed to introduce this small group of monks into the Cistercian Order. But he abandoned it and the Cistercians when, after Easter of 1186, he decided to live as a hermit at Petra Lata, in the hills of Calabria. An unexpected affluence of disciples led him to go further away in the Sela mountains, where he established a new monastic family around San Giovanni in Fiore in 1191. The San Giovanni evoked by the title of the monastery was the visionary of Patmos.

Denounced by the Cistercians as a "fugitive," Joachim exhibited an uncanny talent to secure protection. He knew the ways of the world, and he was remarkably successful as he lobbied the powerful in Church and in State. On the ecclesiastical side, Joachim met Pope Lucius III (1181-1185) in 1184 at Elora, a short distance from Casamari. Lucius encouraged him to write a commentary on the Apocalypse and his major book, *Liber concordiae novi ac veteris testamenti.* In 1186 Joachim visited Lucius's successor, Urban III (1185-1187), in Verona. Urban apparently urged him to go on with his work. After the brief pontificate of Gregory VIII (October-November 1187) Joachim visited Clement III (1187-1191) in Rome in 1188. In June of that year the pope wrote him a laudatory letter. In August 1196 Celestine III (1191-1198) officially recognized the Order of Fiore as distinct from the Cistercian Order.

Joachim also showed an unexpected political wisdom in his relations with imperial and royal powers. In early 1191 at Messina he had an interview with Richard the Lyon-hearted (king, 1189-1199) who was on his way to the crusade. With the English king he seems to have discussed the Apocalypse and the Antichrist. He viewed the events of his times as bordering on the eschaton. Even though the abbot occasionally compared the Holy Empire with Babylon, he also obtained the protection of the Hohenstaufen dynasty. In 1191, in 1194, and again in 1196 he met with Emperor Henry VI (1190-1197). Although he blamed the emperor for waging war against the kingdom of Sicily, Henry VI became a benefactor of his Order. Joachim also knew the empress, Cosenza, whose confession he is reported to have heard on the same occasion. At Palermo in March 1200 he visited their orphaned son, the future Frederick II (emperor, 1215-1250), who also was generous toward the Order of Fiore at the very moment when he was at war with the pope. Meanwhile, Joachim was also in touch with the Norman king of Sicily, Tancred de Hauteville (king, 1184-1194), who donated the land for the foundation of San Giovanni. Hermit and holy man though he wished to be, Joachim kept his finger on the pulse of the broader society, and he was skilled in political maneuvers.

The boldness of Joachim's relations with the powerful was only one aspect of his self-understanding as a monastic reformer. As he reminisced about his pilgrimage to Jerusalem, during which he apparently experienced his first visions, he did not hesitate to compare Calabria with Palestine, San Giovanni in Fiore with Jerusalem, himself with king David. In his fervent imagination the pregnancy of the Cistercian Order, as it gave birth to the Fiorensians, could be compared with

Mary's pregnancy with the Holy Child. As Joachim imagined himself a new Moses, his visions played the role of the burning Bush. He also thought of himself as a new Benedict, and his migration from Corazzo to Petra Lata and hence to the Sela range paralleled Benedict's move from Subiaco to Monte Cassino. "Behold," his first biographer had him say, "with Moses I lead my little sheep into the interior reaches of the desert[1]."

Joachim's monastic foundation was, in his mind, the harbinger of a profound reform of the Church. Although the abbot never said it in so many words, the *figurae*, or analogies, that illustrated his conceptions, pointed to the Fiorensians as the Order of the eschaton, the Latter-Day Saints. The Church was about to enter the last age of the world. It would soon be patterned on Joachim's dream of the highest monastic life, in keeping with a highly elaborate doctrine of the Church and a Trinitarian model that Joachim developed carefully. The most problematic point in the traditional teaching about the Three Persons lay in the understanding of the Holy Spirit. Precisely, while Joachim professed to abide entirely by the Latin tradition and he constantly affirmed the eternity and co-equality of the Three, he had a new perspective on the presence and influence of the Holy Spirit in the created world.

*

After the doctrine of the Trinity had been determined by the great patristic councils, there had only been, in the Latin Church before the time of Joachim, two major debates on the Trinitarian conception of God. The first turned around the *Filioque*, the still unresolved question between the Latin Catholics and the Eastern Orthodox. When pope Benedict VIII (1012-1024), in 1014, crowned Emperor Henry II (973-1024), he endorsed the addition of *Filioque* to the Creed, that had been refused by his predecessors. He thus ignored the anathema of the Council of Chalcedon against those who would "compose another faith" than was formulated in the symbols of Nicaea and Constantinople. For reasons that were no less political than theological, this addition was already enforced in the empire of the Franks, and it had been defended in the *Libri carolini* of the Council of Frankfurt (796). Theologically, the addition safeguarded the pneumatology of Augustine in books VI and XVII of the *De Trinitate,* where the Spirit was identified as the mutual *dilectio* of the Father and the Son[2]. Originally made in Spain, the addition was presumably directed, at the beginning, against Priscillian. It also served to combat the Arianism of the Wisigoths. Politically, however, it was intended to underline the moral superiority of the Latins over the Greeks, at a time when the very existence of an *imperium francorum,* that included the primatial city of Rome, challenged the self-understanding of the older *imperium romanorum* centered in Constantinople, the New Rome.

The addition of the *Filioque* to the Creed was nonetheless uncanonical, and it ran against the entire Greek tradition. That Benedict VIII endorsed it seems all the more extraordinary as he himself was of Greek origin, a member of the notorious Theophylact family, which, through the intrigues of Theodora and her daughter Marozia, had largely controlled the papacy at the end of the ninth century and the beginning of the tenth[3]. While Benedict's acceptance of the *Filioque* may have been prompted by entirely non-dogmatic reasons, it had far-reaching sequels that no pope, presumably, could have foreseen. The rivalry between Greek and Latin theologies reached critical proportions when the patriarch of Constantinople, Photius (c.820-c.893), denounced the *Filioque* as a heresy[4].

The second controversy flared up in 850 between Hincmar (d. 882), archbishop of Reims, and the Saxon monk Gottschalk (d. 869). This time, the debate turned around the formula, *trina deitas,* the orthodoxy of which Gottschalk defended when Hincmar forbade its use in hymns, because, the archbishop said, it implied three divinities[5]. Gottschalk responded that it implied no such thing, and that the archbishop's Latin was defective. The sharp discussion between the two of them, however, had no sequels after Gottschalk died in the monastery of Orbais. Apart from Hincmar the Frankish bishops were not interested in the question. The issue was quickly forgotten, and the problematic formula remained in use. It even appeared later in one of the Eucharistic hymns attributed to Thomas Aquinas. Gottschalk's theology, however, did not deserve oblivion. It raised a question that has not been satisfactorily answered. The monk insisted that deity or divinity should, like goodness and oneness, be treated as an attribute of God. Nobody in the ninth century noticed that, if this is correct, being itself may also be considered, along with the other transcendentals (oneness, goodness, and beauty), an attribute of the divinity. It then follows that the divine Essence, in the inseparable threeness of its oneness (*trina deitas*), cannot be simply identical with any of its attributes. God is ultimately beyond being and goodness and unity and beauty, and is rather "That" which makes these four transcendentals, along with the infinite number of the divine attributes, simultaneously potential and actual, unknown and known to us. Human thought is then plunged in the linguistic paradox that it has to use "is" to say what God is not as well as what God is. In the process, theism becomes sister to non-theism, which also has to use "is" to say, "is not." Although Gottschalk was not equipped to realize it, his apophatic orientation placed his theology on the threshold of a possible dialogue with buddhology and the Buddha.

A less immediately momentous disagreement on the Trinity flared up in Joachim's own century, when, in 1148, Bernard of Clairvaux (c.1090-1153) accused Gilbert de la Porrée (1076-1164), bishop of Poitiers, of tritheism. Gilbert, of course, did not believe in three Gods. He regarded the divine nature or essence as a mere concept since it does not exist apart from the Persons, who alone are real. But if, as St. Bernard argued, the divine Essence as such is not real, then there is nothing common to the Three Persons, and each one is necessarily one God. Hence the accusation of tritheism. As he defended himself at the provincial council of Reims, in March 1148, in the presence of pope Eugene III (1145-1153), Gilbert was not condemned for heresy. Of four points of his teaching that were discussed at the synod only the first was corrected, though, one must admit, rather obscurely: No division must be made in God between Person and nature, so that "God must not be said to be a divine Essence in the ablative sense only, but also in the nominative sense[6]." The ablative sense would make the divine Essence an abstraction; the nominative sense makes each named Person the Essence itself. Thus the Three Persons have to be one and the same real Essence in order to be one God. Bernard's efforts to have the bishop of Poitiers formally declared a heretic failed when his *Professio fidei contra Gilbertum Porretam* was not approved by the pope. Although this was a minor controversy at the time, it is relevant to the Joachimite question for two reasons. Firstly, as we shall see at the end of the present chapter, it came back to life in a different form when Joachim accused Peter Lombard of making God a quaternity. Secondly, it set a precedent that was followed by Lateran Council IV and the popes of the thirteenth century, when they rejected Joachim's criticism of Peter Lombard without finding him guilty of heresy.

*

The Trinitarian problem that emerged in the thirteenth century was occasioned by Joachim's unusual theories about the relations between the Old and the New Testament. The abbot was an occasional visionary. His main visions occurred when he traveled in Palestine and when he resided at Casamari. Whatever their exact nature, moments of profound insight played a major role in his writings. He himself wrote:

> I, Joachim, around, I think, the middle of the silence of the night, and the time when our Lyon of the tribe of Judah is believed to have risen from the dead, suddenly, as I meditated on some points, a revelation, perceived by the eyes of the mind with clarity of understanding, was made to me concerning the fullness of knowledge of this book and the full concord, that I perceived, of the Old and the New Testament[7].

In medieval Latin the word *revelatio* was vague enough to cover inspirations, psychological intuitions, intellectual insights, decisions of councils, as well as the formally revealed doctrines inherited from the Apostles and officially transmitted by the Church. Whatever strength Joachim gave to the word as he recorded his discovery, he never doubted that his exegetical method, the *concordia*, had come to him as a supernatural gift. It enabled him, as he thought, to unveil the meaning of history through an elaborate analysis of the New Testament and of the Church, in light of the beginning and the end, the Old Testament and the Apocalypse.

In spite of his marked mystical strain, Joachim's chief contribution lay in the speculative area. Instead of turning his intellectual powers, like Peter Lombard, to theological analysis and patristic investigation, or, like Abelard, to the reconciliation of diverging canons, the abbot applied them to the realm of symbolism and imagination. He did so with such enthusiasm and dedication, not to say stubbornness, that he had the greatest difficulties remaining within the bounds of traditional orthodoxy. Unlike most of the monastic commentators on the Scriptures, he did not read the text chiefly to express or promote piety. He went far beyond the instructions given in the Rule of St. Benedict, where *lectio divina*, the personal reading and study of Scripture, is entirely subordinate to *opus Dei*, the community's chanting of the inspired Psalms to the praise of God. His eager concern was to discover how the text reveals the truth of the world. In order to find this out Joachim needed ways of reading that were out of the ordinary.

*

As formulated in the *Liber de concordia*, these ways were framed in a typology that implied a drastic reinterpretation of the Augustinian view of history. As he concluded his long work on the City of God, Augustine had summed up the history of the world in six ages, two until Abraham, three more until the coming of Christ, the sixth stretching from Christ to the end of the world. A seventh age corresponded to the Creator's repose after the work of the six days, and it symbolized an eschatological duration that runs parallel to time[8]. In other places of his writings Augustine had compared these historical periods and what were then taken to be the six periods of human life. Parsing the times differently, he had also found six ages in the Old Testament and six in the New, which allowed him to see the Old Testament as a typology and prophecy of the New, and, by the same token, the old Israel as a prophetic image of the Church of Christ. Such a diversity suggests that in Augustine's eyes neither six nor seven was absolute. They were convenient numbers by which to divide long eras into shorter periods, that were sufficiently diverse to allow for flexible development, and small enough for a series of events to be easily memorized. Augustine's historical schema was used in the eleventh and twelfth centuries, notably by Rupert of Deutz[9] (c.1070-1129) and Anselm of Havelberg[10] (d.1158), who made it a framework for an overview of the development of doctrine.

In Joachim's version, however, the ages of the world, six in the Old Testament and six in the New, are more than historical periods. Each group of six constitutes a *status*, a term which, in the language of the twelfth and thirteenth centuries, connotes a certain fullness. A *status* is a state of perfection, even if it is temporary and must eventually give way to a fuller *status*, a higher perfection. Joachim ventured further than the unveiling of analogies between the Old and the New. Where such analogies did not come easily to mind, he was not satisfied with allegorizing the meaning of words and events, as was commonly done, since the *Moralia in Job* of Gregory the Great (540-604), in monastic theology. The correspondences between the Testaments that he sought for had to be literal, since, being the work of God, each Testament must be perfect and complete in itself, while it can also relate to the other by reflecting it as in a mirror. In the Old Testament Joachim therefore discovered numerous types of things to come that pointed to the New. And in turn he read the New Testament as pointing to the eschatological fulfillment of all things that was prefigured in the Apocalypse. So far, this was not at variance with the Benedictine tradition of *lectio divina*. Joachim, however, ventured further when he boldly announced that the correspondence of the two Testaments would soon be more openly manifest, in a future gospel that he called the gospel of the Holy Spirit. This correspondence, *concordia*, was thus unveiled by a convergence of several factors: an amplification of the senses of Scripture, a biblical exegesis centered on the seven seals of Apocalypse 5, 1-5, an exaltation of monasticism, and Trinitarian analogies. This complicated hermeneutic functioned in several modes.

A first mode is symbolized by the Greek letter *alpha*. The phases of history are then related to the divine Persons. The Old Testament was the age of the Father, of the Law, and of human fatherhood, when the Synagogue, which was a Church of married laity, flourished. It was followed by the age of the Word Incarnate and the Spirit, in a New Testament that Joachim dated from the access of Josiah to kingship in the Southern Kingdom (2 Kings 22), around 640. This was the age of the clerical Church, dominated by priests. Then the age of the Spirit will dawn, and the present Church, passing from a clerical to a monastic *status,* will acquire a new type of perfection.

In another mode of typification there are only two periods, of sixty-three generations each. The first goes from Adam to Christ. The second, partly overlapping the first, stretches from king Josiah and the prophet Elijah (though they were not contemporary, Josiah coming some two centuries after Elijah!) to the end of the world. Each generation lasting some thirty years, Joachim calculated that the age of the Spirit would dawn around the year 1260.

*

One would logically expect Joachim at this point to delve into the related questions of the nature of Law and the purpose of the Decalogue. Christian commentaries on the Decalogue already had a long history. From the Carolingian Renaissance to the end of the fourteenth century a number of theologians had studied the principles of morality in terms of the Sinaitic Law. Their treatises were usually brief, but they at least showed a concern both for the principles of moral behavior and for the continuing relevance of the Mosaic revelation. Under Charlemagne, Alcuin (c.730-804) had commented on the Decalogue.

Peter Damian (c.1007-1072) had presented the Ten Commandments as a God-given remedy for the ten plagues of Egypt, and this could be taken allegorically as implying a divine remedy to all subsequent ills of human society. In the four chapters of his *Institutiones in decalogum legis dominicae*, Hugh of St. Victor (c.1096-1141) had noted the distinction between the two tables of the Law and the orientation of both toward the order of charity. Peter Lombard had studied the Ten Commandments in distinctions 37 to 40 of Book III of his *Sentences*. As this became the basic textbook for the Schoolmen's commentaries, it ensured that Law had a degree of prominence in scholastic teaching. As it turned out, however, Peter Lombard was regarded by Joachim as the chief adversary of the sort of monastic theology that the abbot was practicing. In light of the *concordia*, the Mosaic Law could have no meaning in itself. Like the entire Old Testament, the revelation of God the Father, it could only be an obscure prophecy of the New, unintelligible in its time, whose true meaning was manifested by the Gospel of Christ, when it became fully intelligible as meaning what Christ revealed.

Joachim's approach had no success among the professors of theology. A younger contemporary of the abbot, Guillaume d'Auvergne (c.1180-1249), himself a professor at the University who was made bishop of Paris in 1228, composed a *De legibus* and a *Summa de virtutibus et vitiis*, both of which implied that the Decalogue and the Law were intrinsically valid, and not only because of the Gospel. In fact the thirteenth century saw the appearance of specific tractates on Law outside the Commentaries on the Sentences. That discussion of the Christian value of the Mosaic law in its moral and its ritual dimensions was widespread in the twelfth and thirteenth centuries was in part due to political and moral questions about the status of Jews in Christian kingdoms. Politically, the princes were interested in finding sources of easy money. The ensuing moral question,—is it lawful to seize Jewish assets when the prince is in need?—forced out the theological question: What is the status of Jews and Judaism after the coming of the Messiah? Questions of morality and the problem of Judaism came to be mixed, and generally, as we shall see, to the detriment of Jews.

The first Franciscan lecturer at the University, Alexander of Hales, showed a keen interest in the theology of justice and justification. His *Disputed Questiones antequam esset frater*, before he entered the Franciscan Order, discussed the justice of the Old Law and its fulfilment in Christ[8] as well as the "justification of the impious[11]." After he became a Franciscan in 1235 his *Glossa in quatuor libros sententiarum* distinguished four kinds of laws: the rule of the natural will, the law of grace, which rules the higher part of reason, the Mosaic law, which rules the lower part of reason, and the law of the flesh or sensual will, which is responsible for sin[12]. Progressively unobserved in the early Church, the Mosaic Law was now definitely abolished. Alexander's disciple Jean de la Rochelle, master regent in 1236, composed a *Brevis explanatio praeceptorum* before 1235. He was also largely responsible for putting together the *Summa fratris Alexandri*, a compilation of writings from early Franciscan theologians and others. This composition contains the longest of all medieval tractates on Law. It examines at great length the Eternal Law, the Natural Law, the Mosaic Law and the Evangelical Law [13]. The treatment of the Law of Moses includes a detailed examination, of the ten commandments.

An interest in Law continued to characterize Franciscan theology. Robert Grosseteste (c.1175-1253), bishop of Lincoln in 1235, was not himself a Franciscan, but he was close to the Friars and he lectured at their English studium. He composed a *De decem mandatis* around 1230, that he followed with a *De cessatione legis* after 1231[14]. Between 1228 and 1235 Grosseteste wrote an exegetical and theological commentary on the *Hexaëmeron* that had a part in the inspiration of Bonaventure's later lectures on the same topic[15]. In the last decades of the thirteenth century Matthew de Aquasparta (c.1237-1302), who like Bonaventure taught in Paris, was Master general of the Order, and became a cardinal, included a discussion *de legibus* in his Disputed questions. He divided Law in five kinds, eternal, natural, scriptural, Mosaic, and evangelical[16]. These developments show that Joachim's view of the Law, and by implication his *concordia*, were disregarded in the approach to theology and ethics that prevailed in the theological schools in the decades that followed him.

Born of an idiosyncratic reading of the letter of Scripture, Joachim's theories amounted to symbolic interpretations of the spiritual status of humankind, which were themselves illuminated by an inconsistent mixture of several types of spiritual senses, and by the projection on the expected future of a monastic utopia nurtured by nostalgia for a pure Church run by monks. In the Apocalypse, that Joachim took as the key to all Scripture, Joachim read about the coming of a monastic and contemplative Church that will arise in response to a new revelation. His readers could easily infer that the three perfections of the Church amounted to three successive Churches, an inference, however, that Joachim himself never explicitly formulated.

*

Joachim correctly saw the doctrine of the Trinity as the very heart of the Christian revelation. It was, he believed, by applying Trinitarian principles to the reading of Scripture that one could discover its meaning. He however added that, just as the reign of the Father was superseded by that of the Son, the reign of the Son must be succeeded by that of the Spirit. And just as the three divine Persons are one by nature and they always act together, so the two testaments must be complemented and perfected by a third, the yet unrevealed gospel of the Holy Spirit, which will necessarily be the last and eternal Gospel, since there is no other divine Person beyond the Third. History can then be characterized as a process of spiritualization. Soon the Church will reach its highest state or perfection in a recovered virginity that will be the fruit of the Spirit. It will cease to be clerical and will become monastic. The dominant impact of the Spirit will follow that of the Father in the revelation to the Patriarchs and that of the Son in the Incarnation. The Eternal Gospel will reveal and manifest the ultimate perfection called for by the Old and by the New Testament.

In the Joachimite perspective the Holy Trinity, perfect in itself, is experienced on earth as one kingdom that evolves in three stages. The letter of the Old Testament projected the image of the Father at work in it; the letter of the New has shown the image of the Son Incarnate; and the spiritual understanding of both will soon lead to the image of the Spirit. While Joachim affirmed the equality and co-eternity of the Three Persons, his presentation leaned toward a final predominance of the Third over the First and the Second. It looks as though, by affirming that two Persons contribute to the Spirit, the doctrine of the *Filioque* sees the Spirit as a fulfillment of the One who proceeds, by generation, from one only, and of the One who does not proceed.

*

Joachim speculated on the six days of creation in chapters 3 to 29 of Book V of the *Liber concordiae*. As the preface of this writing indicates, book One deals with "the judgments of God in the Old Testament and the seven wars of the sons of Israel[17]," book Two with "the chief loci of the concord of the Old and the New Testament, that occurred along certain decades of generations[18], and the one spiritual meaning that marvelously proceeds from the two letters." Book Three examines "several kinds of sabbaths, other loci of the *concordia* of the Testaments, and their opening of marvelous understandings of future events." Book Four studies the generations that go from Adam to John the Baptist, and from king Osiah to the prophet Elijah[19]. Book Five, which is by itself longer than the first four books, unfolds the spiritual meaning of the main stories of the Old Testament, from which "many future events are shown to us, if we understand them spiritually."

The first of these stories is, not surprisingly, the creation in six days, or, as Joachim, counting the sabbath, says, "the seven original days."

These will be explained "according to the allegorical understanding," which at this point is divided in five kinds: historical, moral, tropological, contemplative, and anagogical. Joachim intends to elucidate the *Hexaëmeron* in a sevenfold "confession" of the Trinity. The first confession is of the Father, the second of the Son, the third of the Spirit, the fourth of the Father and the Son, the fifth of the Father and the Spirit, the sixth of the Son and the Spirit, the seventh of the Father and the Son and the Spirit[20].

This ascent from the Father to the unity of the Three Persons is presumed to unveil a "typological understanding" of Scripture (*intelligentia typica*) that will be divided in seven meanings. If to these seven meanings one adds the five allegorical senses already mentioned, one obtains twelve senses, twelve being the perfect number of the "loaves of proposition" which, before Solomon's Temple was built, were placed on the altar[21]! For brevity's sake, says Joachim, the twelve senses may be reduced to four, the main ones actually containing the others. These are: "historical, moral, contemplative,—under which name two are contained, tropological and anagogical, the former inferior, the latter superior,—and typical, which is divided in seven kinds ." This amounts to one meaning for each divine Person, plus a fourth one for the Three together. In principle, therefore, each of the days of creation supports a ladder of four senses, that can be further multiplied into twelve. Joachim, as one can see here, was not shy of delving into what he called elsewhere "a certain power of spiritual arithmetic[22]." In chapter 2 Joachim shows how the system functions: He finds twelve meanings of the story of Sara and Hagar. As he surveys the seven days of creation, however, he seems to get tired of his own game. He looks only for four sets of meanings. And when he comes to the fourth he simply refers back to the first, thereby unwittingly undermining his distinction of seven levels of meaning, which is largely artificial, and more conceptual than real.

What, then, is the Joachimite understanding of the six days of creation? Joachim's explanations amount to repetitious and not very original typological analyses of the Old Testament. These analyses are dominated by a sevenfold "confession" of the Three Persons. For it is not enough, for the abbot of Fiore, to confess the Three Persons and their unity. One should also confess the Persons two by two. Each of these successive confessions is alleged to open one typological sense. Rather than being focused on the story of Christ in the New Testament, however, this exercise follows the march of the world, through seven periods of ten generations each, to the trials that will herald the time of judgment. This future event, that Joachim believes imminent, will introduce the millennium, a kingdom that will last a thousand years. Alluding to the "days" of the prophet Daniel (Dan. 12, 9-16), Joachim exclaims:

> 1. Blessed is he who expects and who reaches day one thousand three hundred and thirty-three. One thing I say in all security: These mysteries being fulfilled, the seventh angel will blow the trumpet; under him all the sacred written mysteries will be fulfilled; and there will be a time of peace in the whole earth.
>
> As to the elucidation of the mystery of this number, let no one push me! Let no one force me to go beyond the assigned boundary! For God has the power to make his mysteries still clearer[23].

*

With his speculations on the Church of the Spirit Joachim was, unwittingly, it would seem, lighting a time bomb. In the mild way of a pious scholar eager to explore the Scriptures, he was adamantly opposed to the rational theology that was emerging in the schools, and determined to renovate monastic theology through his method of biblical reading. One of his chief targets was, precisely, Peter Lombard (d.c.1160), the father of scholastic theology. The point he selected for his attack on the Lombard was highly sensitive, since the bishops and popes could hardly remain indifferent: the doctrine of the Holy Trinity. Joachim accused the Lombard of teaching that the Three Persons exist in addition to the reality (*res*) of their common Essence, thus making the Trinity a quaternity. With his critique of the author of what would soon become the standard textbook of scholasticism, Joachim undermined the intellectual enterprise that became the glory of the thirteenth century. As he did so he correctly discerned a latent danger that threatens Trinitarian theology: so to reify the divine Essence that it seems to stand over against the Persons and the Persons relate to It instead of simply being It, and the Essence being, reversely, the Persons. As Bernard had insisted against Gilbert de la Porrée, the divine Essence is real and not merely notional. This, however, makes it easy for a certain type of mind, that tends to understand language univocally, to see the Essence as really distinct from the Persons, and thus to conceive the Trinity as a quaternity.

This was precisely what Joachim accused Peter Lombard of doing. But was Joachim's reading of Peter Lombard correct? Events were soon to show, at the fourth Council of the Lateran, that Innocent III (pope, 1198-1216) was especially concerned, if not about Joachim's theology as a whole, at least about the abbot's critique of the Lombard. On the pope's instructions Lateran Council IV carefully examined Joachim's criticism and, declaring Peter Lombard orthodox in his Trinitarian theology, condemned it. The condemnation, however, was strictly limited to this point. While it drew the attention of theologians to a major flaw in the abbot's thinking, it did nothing to mitigate the growing popularity of his apocalyptic expectations.

Notes

1 Wessley, Joachim..., p. 83 and note 18 of chapter 4; all the above analogies are abundantly illustrated in this book.

2 *De Trinitate*, VI, v, 7 (Bibliothèque Augustinienne, vo1.15, Paris: Desclée de Brouwer, p. 484); XV, xvii, 29 (BA, vol. 16, p.504).

3 All the popes from Sergius III (894-911) to John XII (955-964),—who was deposed by a synod in 963 for flagrant immorality, and assassinated the following year,—were related to, or creatures of, the Theophylact family; Benedict VIII was himself a great-grandson of Marozia.

4 From time to time theologians of the West composed a *Contra errores graecorum*, a large part of which defended the orthodoxy of the Augustinian doctrine that the Holy Spirit «proceeds from the Father and from the Son as from one principle,» and explicitly or implicitly condemned as false the doctrine of patriarch Photius that the *ekporeusis* of the Spirit is from the Father alone. Thomas Aquinas himself wrote such a pamphlet: *Contra errores Graecorum, ad Urbanum IV papam maximum* (Pierre Mandonnet, ed., *Thomae Aquinatis opuscula omnia*, vol. 3, Paris: Lethielleux, 1927, Opusculum XXVII, p. 279-328; on the Filioque, p.304-318).

5 *De una et non trina deitate* (*Patrologia latina*, 125,473-618); see Jean Devisse, *Hincmar, Archevêque de Reims, 845-882*, 3 vol., Geneva: Droz, 1975, vol. I, p. 154- 186; George H. Tavard, *Trina Deitas. The Controversy between Hincmar and Gottschalk*, Milwaukee: Marquette University Press, 1996. The formula, *trina deitas*, that Hincmar considered heretical, is close to

trina unitas, that was used in a pontifical document, the *Fides Pelagii*, sent by Pope Pelagius I (pope, 556-561) in February 557 to the Merovingian king Childebert I (king of Burgundy, 534-558). *Trina unitas* is still used in the *Catechism of the Catholic Church*, New York: Doubleday, 1995, n. 253-254, p.75.

6 *De primo tantum Romanus Pontifex definivit, ne aliqua ratio in theologia inter naturam et personam divideret, neve Deus divina essentia diceretur ex sensu ablativi tantum, sed etiam nominativi* (See Denzinger-Schönmetzer, *Enchiridion symbolorum,* ed. xxxii, Barcelona: Herder, 1963, n. 745).

7 *Ego Joachim circa medium ut opiner noctis silentium ad hora qua Leo noster de tribu Juda resurrexisse estimatur a mortuis, subito mihi meditanti aliqua, quadam mentis oculis intelligentiae claritatis percepta, de plenitudine scientiae hujus libri et de tota percepta veteris ac novi testamenti concordia, revelatio facta est* (*Liber concordiae*, fol. 2C).

8 *De Civitate Dei*, bk XXII, 30 (BA vo1.37, 1959, p.716).

9 *De Trinitate et operibus ejus libri XLII* (PL 167).

10 *Dialogi* (PL 188,1119-1243).

11 Q. XX: *De justitia legis veteris* (*Questiones disputatae antequam esset frater*, 3 vol., Quaracchi, 1960, vol. 1, 1960, p. 359-373); Q. XXI: *De adimpletione legis per Christum* (p. 373-386).

12 *Glossa in quatuor libros sententiarum* (*Bibliotheca franciscana medii aevi*, vol. XVI, Quaracchi, 1952, p. 308).

13 Bk III, part II: *De legibus et praeceptis* (*Summa Fratris Alexandri*, Quaracchi, 1948, p. 314-939).

14 Richard Dales and Edward B. King, eds., *De decem praeceptis*, Oxford University Press, 1987; *De cessatione legalium*, Oxford University Press, 1986.

15 Richard Dales and Servus Gieben, *Robert Grosseteste. Commentary on the Hexaëmeron:* Oxford University Press, 1982.

16 A sixth investigation asked if, given the evangelical law, observance of the Mosaic law is still permissible (Matthieu de Aquasparta, *Quaestiones disputatae de anima separata, de anima beata, de jejunio, et de legibus*, Quaracchi: Collegio Sancti Bonaventurae, 1959; *de legibus*: p. 431-571).

17 Since the numbering of the folios starts at chapter 1, this comes just before folio I.

18 A decade, in this context, would be a series of ten generations.

19 Since Elijah came before Osiah, *revelatio Helie* must designate the identification of the Baptist as the Elijah who was to come just before the Messiah.

20 Ch. 2, fol. 61B.

21 1 Samuel 21, 4-6.

22 Ch.2, fol.61C: ...*quaedam arithmeticae spiritualis virtute...* (*Enchiridion super Apocalypsim,* Toronto: Pontifical Institute of Medieval Studies, 1986, p. 82).

23 Ch.118, fol.135B.

Chapter 2
Gherardo

When Lateran Council IV met on 14 November 1215 it proceeded, following a mandate from Pope Innocent III, to condemn Joachim's contention that Peter Lombard's theology presented God as a quaternity rather than a trinity. Eventually the abbot's theological method and system escaped explicit condemnation, even though the decree that was adopted by the council (Constitution 2: *De errore abbatis Joachim*) blamed Joachim's critique of the Lombard on an erroneous methodology. Joachim was said to infer that in God there is not one reality (*res*), or essence, or substance, or nature, which is the Father and the Son and the Holy Spirit. While the abbot conceded that Father, Son, Spirit are one essence, one substance, and one nature, he regarded this unity, not as a true and proper oneness, but rather as a collective union based on similarities, just as many men may be said to be one people, and many believers one Church. In other words, Joachim was found guilty of making an illegitimate induction from the natural unity of the human race to the divine unity of the Three Persons. His conception of the Trine Unity was warped by its model, the co-existence of three men, and the Trinity was thereby implicitly reduced to an anthropological projection. In the course of its explanation the Council stated a principle that has remained classical, regarding the analogy between the creation and God: "...between the Creator and the creature there cannot be noticed so great a similarity that a greater dissimilarity between them must not be noticed[1]." It follows that the unity of the Three Persons as one divine Being is more unlike than like the oneness of the human race.

This principle has been better remembered in Catholic theology than Joachim's error regarding Peter Lombard and its solemn condemnation. Whether Joachim understood or misunderstood Peter is, in the long run, of little moment, though it would have been of major importance if indeed the theology of the Schools had been based on an erroneous understanding of the divine oneness. Given the defective methodology that Lateran IV denounced, however, it is surprising that the council made no critical comment on Joachim's history of the Church, on the *concordia* between the two Testaments and their relative obsolescence, on his expectation of the imminent irruption of an Eternal Gospel, on the notion that three periods of the Church result from successive input by the Three Persons, and on the association of a perfect, monastic, Church with the Spirit rather than with the Father and the Son.

*

In spite of the strictures of the Lateran Council on Joachim's theology, the memory of the Calabrian abbot was protected by several sets of factors. Firstly, Joachim was a famous seer, and the hierarchy's attitude to visionaries, in the twelfth and thirteenth centuries, and in fact up to the Reformation, was notably ambiguous. The Roman Inquisition, and still more the Spanish Inquisition, were not lenient toward seers whose visions were associated with heterodox doctrines. Bishops and popes, however, not uncommonly protected and even consulted visionaries who had a reputation of holiness and orthodoxy. This openness to extraordinary communications from God was instrumental in the fame of several women mystics who corresponded with bishops and popes. Such were, roughly contemporary with Joachim, Hildegard of Bingen (1109-1179) and Elizabeth of Schönau (1129-1164). In the thirteenth century there were the Béguine, later Cistercian, Mechtild of Magdeburg (1212-c.1282), the Cistercian Gertrude of Helfta (1256-1302), and, with a more limited range, the Béguine Marie d'Oignies (c.1177-1213), the English Recluse Christina of Markyate (c.1196-after 1266), Beatrice of Nazareth (1200-1268), Mechtild of Hackeborn (1241-1299). Others, however, became innocent victims when some Inquisitors suspected them of belonging in one way or another to the movement of the Free Spirit in the Netherlands or, later, to the Alhumbrados of Spain, The great Marguerite Porete (c.1250-1310) was such a victim. And, far from protecting her, Jeanne d'Arc's voices and visions were to be featured in her indictment by the bishop of Bauvais in 1430. Willingness to listen to contemporary prophets, however, may have been decisive for the encouragement that Joachim received from pope Lucius III, although Lucius was hardly permissive toward sectarian groups. He personally presided over the synod of Verona (1184), which anathematized "every heresy," namely, the Cathars, Patarini, Humiliati, Poor of Lyon, Passagini, Josepini, Arnaldisti. Moreover, Celestine III (1191-1198), who in 1196 approved the foundation of Fiore, was the immediate predecessor of Innocent III, the pope of the Fourth Lateran Council.

Secondly, Joachim had repeatedly insisted that the Three Persons have full equality and eternity. In so doing he had directly, and presumaly unwittingly, undermined the assumption of his own ecclesiology. In the light of the authentic Trinitarian doctrine it is wrong to assert, as he did, that the three historical states which the Church, as he taught, must undergo, and the perfections that correspond to each of them, reflect the divine Persons' manifestations on earth. He should rather have acknowledged that in its historical institutional reality the Church is more unlike than like the Kingdom of Heaven in God.

Thirdly, the abbot of Fiore had expressed his eagerness to subject all his works, at least posthumously, to the judgment of the Apostolic See. This instruction was formally written in 1200, in a moving letter addressed to the other abbots of the Order of Fiore. It was explicitly mentioned at the end of the decree of the Lateran Council: "He ordered all his writings to be sent to us, to be approved or corrected according to the judgment of the apostolic see, when he dictated a letter, that he signed with his own hand, in which it is firmly professed that he holds the faith that is held by the Roman Church, which is, by the Lord's disposition, the mother and teacher of all the faithful[2]."

It is hardly surprising that this letter ensured Joachim's place in the eyes of the bishops of Rome once he had passed away. It was a warm, unambiguous assertion of their doctrinal authority. Joachim's writings must be presented to "the apostolic summit," to "him to whom the magisterium has been universally given[3]." He blames the troubles of the times for the fact that he himself has only presented one, the *Concordia*. But if he dies before presenting the others, "so that they be corrected if anything is there that should be corrected (which I do not deny is there, though I am not aware of anything such)," his brother Fiorensian abbots must present them to Rome without delay. The letter includes a strong affirmation of the Roman primacy, toward which the writer has "devotion and fidelity." He declares himself to be

> always prepared to observe what it has stated or will state, not to defend his own opinion against its holy faith, totally believing what it believes..., rejecting what it rejects, receiving what it receives; firmly believing that the gates of Hell cannot prevail against it, and if for a time it happens to be troubled and shaken by storms, its faith will not fail until the consummation of the world.

The praise of the Church of Rome and the assertion of its unique privileges occur frequently in Joachim's work. The abbot never altered the position he formulated in his early *Enchiridion super Apocalypsim*, begun between 1183 and 1185. Adherence to the Church of Rome was presented as a condition of church-membership: "What does not adhere to the Roman Church must be banished outside the Church." On this principle he spoke of "the separation (*sessio*) of the Greeks from the Roman Church." He even saw their liturgical practices as major obstacles to the flow of divine grace. And he argued that the Greek corruptions were foreseen in the story of Elijah, read, of course, according to the *concordia*:

> The Sareptan woman was scared by the bread cooked in the ashes and the oil, which designate the pure doctrine of faith and charity that the Latin Church has brought its members, not by the fermented bread and carnal foods that the ravens brought, which designate their much corrupted doctrine, like that of Origen, and their carnal institutions, and the apocryphal scriptures that they receive indifferently, and that they themselves brought and presented, because of which grace left them and was transferred to the Roman Church, the faith of which never fails, and even if it must be shaken like wheat, nevertheless the gates of Hell will not prevail against it.

Again, "in Rome is the general Church who is the mother of all the elect, who, because she is the one and unique Dove of Christ, fecundated by the warmth and the spiritual oil of the Holy Spirit, labors in procreating children for God and educating them spiritually." Joachim asks the rhetorical question: "Which is that one Church that is called the City of the Sun, if not the Church of the Romans, which serves unity and peace to all others, because she is the mother and the link of all the Churches?" So fervent a devotion to the Church of the Romans,—"the spiritual Jerusalem,"—made it difficult indeed for the bishops of Rome to regard the abbot of Fiore as one who promoted false doctrines and made fake prophecies. Leniency and understanding toward the abbot's questionable ideas came to them all the more naturally as they found no reason to disagree with the judgment expressed at the end of the second constitution of Lateran IV, that the monastery of San Giovanni in Fiore was a commendable community of holy observance[4]. This may well have acted as an invitation to shield it from all scandal surrounding the theology of its founder.

*

Forty years after Lateran Council IV the situation had notably deteriorated for the spiritual followers of Joachim. This was mostly due to the reinterpretation of his insights by a young Franciscan from Sicily, Gherardo da Borgo San Donnino (d.1276). This reinterpretation was formulated in a *Liber introductorius ad evangelium aeternum* issued in 1254, that Gherardo himself is said to have peddled in front of the Cathedral of Notre Dame in Paris. It provoked an enormous turmoil at the university of Paris. Gherardo's central idea was simple: The third age of the Church, announced by Joachim, has dawned in St. Francis of Assisi, who was the sixth angel of the Apocalypse (more exactly, the fifth of the angels mentioned after the Lamb has opened the sixth seal). This angel restrains the first four from destroying the earth until the elect have been marked with the sign of the living God (Apo.7). According to Gherardo the 144000 elect, the Latter-day Saints, are no other than the Franciscans, the monastic order that Joachim had announced. The Eternal Gospel, heralded by the primitive Rule of St. Francis, is now being manifested, Joachim's *Liber concordiae* counting as its first book. The year 1260, as foreseen by Joachim, will see the full manifestation of the Eternal Gospel and the formation of the monastic Church.

It can hardly be an excuse for Gherardo's thinking, although it may in part explain it, that other voices in the thirteenth century were also announcing a new age of the Church. There is no evidence that the great Mechtild of Magdeburg was acquainted with Joachimite speculations, though she knew of the controversy around the friars that had erupted at the university of Paris. Like Joachim, however, and possibly reflecting the anxiety of her Dominican confessor, she announced the rise of a new religious order, that she identified as a renovated order of Preachers. More strangely perhaps, Mechtild honored the memory of the controversial emperor Frederick II and of the Hohenstaufen dynasty, themselves, as we have seen, benefactors of the Order of Fiore. She prophesied that Frederick's young grandson, Conradin (d.1268), would be closely associated to the new order and the renewal of the Church. One could not in fact have been more mistaken. Conradin was beheaded on October 29, 1268 by order of his adversary Charles d'Anjou, after he was captured at the battle of Tagliacozzo (August 23, 1268). He had done nothing to promote a spiritual renovation of Christendom.

Other and more dangerous movements emerged in Italy around the fateful year of 1260. From Parma came Gherardo Segarelli (d.1300), an illiterate man whose preaching, which was, apparently, on the vulgar side, met with surprising popularity. He and and his disciples, the Apostoli, announced the imminent coming of the Kingdom of God. Segarelli's successor, Fra Dolcino de Novare (d.1307), was a rabid anti-papal preacher, who literally terrorized parts of Northern Italy at the end of the century. In a book composed in 1316 the Inquisitor Bernard Gui listed twenty grievous errors taken from his teaching, several of which seemed to encourage immoral behavior. No less than four military expeditions were called to destroy the sect. In Milan in the same period another apocalyptic figure, Guillelmina (d.1282), gathered disciples and admirers who, after she died, regarded her as the incarnation of the Holy Spirit.

When a professor in the faculty of Arts at the university of Paris, the secular priest Guillaume de St-Amour (d.1272), refuted Gherardo da Borgo San Donnino, he did not only reject the identification of St. Francis with the angel of the sixth seal. He also identified the advocacy and practice of poverty by the friars as a dangerous heresy. As a university professor and a secular priest he resented the intrusion of Dominicans, under papal protection, into the university, and the extravagant privileges that were granted to the two groups of friars at the expense of the diocesan clergy, against what seemed to be the traditional order of clerical authority. Guillaume de St-Amour spoke for a conservative party of intellectuals in a turmoil that spread far and wide. He accused all the friars of following the radical theories of Gherardo and Joachim. In his polemic, however, he adopted a basic thesis of those he was fighting. He agreed with the Calabrian prophet that the Church in its present state was coming to an end, and that the eschaton was dawning. Far from being the order of the Last Days, however, Dominicans and Franciscans were heralds of Antichrist and portents of the coming end of the world.

*

On the whole, the impact of Joachim di Fiore and of Gherardo da Borgo San Donnino was more affective than intellectual. It was in part for this reason that the Franciscans had a hard time getting rid of it, and all the more so as, unlike the Friars Preacher, they had from the beginning exhibited a fissiparous tendency that led in pretty much all directions. Fidelity to the personal example of Francis could conceivably be compatible with distinctive understandings of evangelical poverty and different forms of apostolic life. Finding the right way was an urgent task for the followers of the Poverello. Bonaventure, as we shall see, played an essential role in this, though the Spiritual Franciscans in the fourteenth century evidently came too late to fall within his horizon.

The Spirituals in their heyday were nonetheless the direct product of the crisis of the thirteenth century, a crisis that was felt in the corridors of spiritual power. Popes were involved. In the long run, the ambiguity of several papal actions had its part of responsibility in the strange happenings that ensued, when a doctrine on the ties between the divine Persons and the Church was held with immunity, even though it was patently opposed to the Catholic tradition regarding the Three Persons.

Notes

1 *...inter Creatorem et creaturam non potest similitudo notari quin inter eos major sit dissimilitudo notanda* (*Conciliorum Oecumenicorum Decreta,* Basle: Herder, 1972, Decree II: *De errore abbatis Joannis*, p. 208, lines 33-34).

2 COD, p. 209, lines 1-5.

3 ... *Quia vero propter angustia temporum non potui hucusque opuscula ipsa, praeter librum Concordiae, Apotolico culmino praesentare ut ab eo corrigerentur si quae ibi (quod non abnuo, etsi mihi conscius non sim) occurrerint corrigenda... omnes libros ei cui datum est omnimode magisterium praesentare rogo ex parte Dei omnipotentis Coabbatos meos... quam citius poterint collecta omnia... Apostolico examini praesentent, recipientes ab eadem Sede vice mea correptionem, et exponentes ei meam circa ipsam devotionem et fidem, et quod ea semper paratus sim quae ipsa statuit vel statuerit observare, nullamque meam opinionem contra ejus defendere sanctam fidem, credens ad integrum quae ipsa credit, ut tam in moribus quam in doctrina correptionem, abjiciens quod ipsa abjicit, suscipiens quod suscipit ipsa, credens firmiter non posse portas inferi praevalere adversus eam; et si ad horam turbari et procellis agitari contingat, non deficere fidem ejus usque ad consummationem seculi.* (Text in the Bollandists' publication, *Acta sanctorum*, May, vol.7, Paris/Rome, 1866, p. 102; the treatment of Joachim is lengthy: p. 87-141; the letter is also reproduced in Daniel, *Liber de concordia...*, p. 4-6).

4 COD, p. 209, line 37-210, line 1.

Chapter 3
The Politics of the Eschaton

The happenings in Calabria and their sequels had a much wider stage than the Southern sections of the Italian peninsula. The political context of Western Christendom formed the horizon of their theological contents, and it was bound to be the scene of their possible implications. Joachim, as we have seen, was himself not innocent of political involvement, since he had dealings, not only with the pope, but also with the emperor, with the king of England on the way to the Crusade, and with the lesser, but no less dangerous personages who aspired to the control of Sicily and Southern Italy. The petty or nobler ambitions of reigning houses and sundry adventurers posed a fundamental problem of discernment regarding what justice called for in the specific circumstances of the times. Moreover, since the thirteenth century was a major period of reawakening for philosophical and theological reflection, the contemporary movements of thought could not be without reference to the political order. Insofar as Joachim and Gherardo envisioned a radical transformation of society, their views of the future questioned the effective shape of Christendom, if not also its very nature. Their prophecies posited an upheaval of the political order that had taken shape over the centuries, out of the ruins of the Roman Empire, through the conflation of remaining Roman structures and incoming Germanic customs.

*

The political order was carefully scrutinized in the theological schools of the thirteenth century. Like everyone at the time, both Thomas Aquinas and Bonaventure were more favorable to a monarchy than to other political systems. They regarded monarchy as more natural and more effective than other regimes. In addition, a monarchy seemed more compatible with the biblical data about the government of the ancient People of God. The Bible, however, included the story of many bad kings. Both theologians were therefore especially concerned lest kings turn into tyrants. In fact, despite the universal predominance of monarchic regimes and the prevailing sense of the unity of Christendom, the map of Western Europe presented a patchwork in regard to the quality of the kings, which varied enormously geographically and chronologically.

In France Louis IX (1214-1270) was highly popular, like his mother Blanche de Castille (1188-1252), who acted as regent in his minority (1226-1234). As regent she had been involved in the crusade against the Cathars. This had begun under Philippe Augustus (1180-1223), and the military operations were led by Simon de Montfort under the guidance of the papal legate, the abbot of Cîteaux Arnaud-Amaury. It was Queen Blanche, however, who imposed the treatise of Meaux on the Count of Toulouse, in March 1229. She again administered the kingdom when her son embarked on the seventh crusade in 1248[1]. Again like his mother, king Louis was a careful administrator of justice, and at the same time unbending in his defense of the privileges of the crown. The situation deteriorated under his son, Philippe III *le Hardi* (1245-1285), a devout man without much common sense[2]. During most of this period the Holy Roman Empire was itself in a precarious shape. Frederick II (1215-1250) was a determined adversary of the popes during most of his long reign. Excommunicated in 1227, he nevertheless took part in the sixth Crusade (1230) with distinction. He even proclaimed himself king of Jerusalem, thus placing Gregory IX (pope, 1227-1241) before a fait accompli that the pope was unable to undo. In 1239 Frederick was again excommunicated when his soldiery invaded papal lands. The popes were led to doubt Frederick's orthodoxy because of his good relations with both Jews and Muslims.

Moreover, in the later decades of the century Southern Italy and Rome were in a turmoil because of Frederick's grandson, Conradin (1252-1268). In 1258, on the invitation of the burghers of Florence, Conradin claimed the crown of Naples and Sicily, against his uncle Manfred (1232-1266), an illegitimate son of Frederick II, who had been made king before he turned against his father. Too young at the time to act effectively, however, Conradin responded in 1266 to a request from several cities that he protect them from Charles d'Anjou (1226-1285), brother of Louis IX of France, to whom Urban IV (pope,

1261-1264) had entrusted the kingdom of Naples[3]. After a few successes and a triumphal reception by the people of Rome, Conradin was captured at the battle of Tagliacozzo. He was beheaded after some kind of trial, on October 29 1268, by order of Charles d'Anjou. The Hohenstaufen line ended with him, stifled in part by the popes' determined opposition to Frederick II and his descendants.

The Crusades were at the center of the foreign policy of every nation. They were in part a reconquest of lands lost to the Muslims several centuries before, in part self-defense against an alien and threatening power, in part altruistic service for the protection of pilgrims. They were also a search for fulfillment of a utopian dream of the Kingdom of God, and many believed them to the beginning of the final battles that would precede the eschaton. In any case, they were bound to fail in the long run, for the simple reason that they required carving out new principalities that were deprived of natural borders and militarily insecure.

Acting as a devout Christian king of his time and place, Louis IX had taken part in the seventh Crusade with enthusiasm, in spite of his mother's misgivings. He was to die of the plague during the eighth Crusade, an ill-conceived attempt to crush the military power of Islam by attacking Tunis. Though the seventh Crusade was itself a military disaster, the king had brought back from it what, with pious naïveté, he took to be a first-class relic of the Passion of Christ. In 1239 he had acquired "the crown of thorns" from the Latin emperor of Constantinople, Baldwin II (1217-1273). Hard-pressed to keep a battle-ready army to fight the legitimate Greek emperor, Baldwin had pawned his alleged relics of the Passion with the Republic of Venice as down-payment for his debts. The pious king Louis bought them back. In 1241 he acquired more relics, and he ordered the *Sainte Chapelle* built precisely to house these spiritual treasures. The pilgrims who approach the chapel from the side may still notice that it is shaped like a reliquary.

Besides its practical purpose this building had eschatological significance, in more or less loose connection with Joachim's apocalyptic theology. What remained of this theology in the Christian people at large in the second half of the thirteenth century was a vague but disturbing feeling that the Second Coming of Christ was not far off.

It should happen, according to Paul's epistle to the Romans, ch. 11, as commonly understood, after the conversion of the Jews, which itself might take place,—but this was no longer biblical,—after the reconquest of the Holy Land. Precisely, the windows of the *Sainte Chapelle*, as their purport is still visible despite later substantial repairs, illustrate the entire history of the world. On the North side, going toward the sanctuary, five windows depict the Pentateuch, the next two showing Isaiah's prophecy of Christ, the infancy of Jesus, and the gospel of John. Facing them on the South side, six windows illustrate the books of Judith, Job, Esther, and Kings, leading to a seventh window that gives a legendary history of the relics. The Passion of Christ is seen over the altar, along with the Resurrection and the descent of the Spirit at Pentecost. Facing this, the great rose in the Western wall illustrates the Apocalypse[4]. Once they were inside the church, the faithful could therefore feel that they already were, symbolically, beyond the end of time, gathering the promises of all the Scriptures, and tasting the beatific fruits of the two advents of Christ.

*

Given the political conditions and the spiritual context of the Christian kingdoms, it is not surprising that the greatest theologians of the thirteenth century had occasion to debate political questions. Thomas Aquinas was all the more interested in such problems as his commentaries on Aristotle include a study of the first three books of the *Politics*[5]. In 1266 Thomas also composed a more theological treatise for the king of Cyprus, *Tractatus de rege et regno*. The full tractate, as we have it, is very long. Only a short part, however, was written by Thomas himself, the authentic section ending in the middle of Part II, chapter 5. A friend and disciple, the Dominican Ptolemy of Lucca (c.1236-c.1326), completed the treatise at such length that he wrote more than twice as much as Aquinas.

As he presents this opusculum, Marie-Dominique Chenu esteems that social turmoil in Cyprus in the thirteenth century justified Thomas's approval of a strict monarchy, the rule of one good man over many, as the best political system, the rule of an evil man being the worst[6]. The text of Aquinas, however, makes no allusion to such troubles.

One could even gather from it the impression that the kingdom of Cyprus enjoys total peace and tranquility. The tractate is purely theoretical. It argues largely from Scripture. It could have been addressed to any reigning king or queen in Europe without major changes in the argumentation.

Book I explores the nature of kingship, with many examples from the Old Testament and occasional references to Aristotle. *Rex*, the Latin term for king, derives from the verb *regere*, "to rule." It designates the person in charge of *regimen*, the task of organizing and ruling the people. While this task could be entrusted to an aristocracy, to a small elite group, or to the whole people itself or its delegates (a democracy), a monarchy is the best regime, essentially for two reasons. First, only a king can truly imitate God, king of the universe, and be among his people like God in creation and the soul in the human body[7] (ch. 12). Second, only a one-man rule can ensure the unity of the people, a pluriform rule being naturally divided, and the more so as more people take part in government (ch. 1 and 2). The king, however, has the obligation of pursuing virtue in himself and justice in the people. If he does not do so he becomes a tyrant. Although government by one evil ruler is better than government by many evil rulers (ch. 3-5), it is still unjust oppression. Thomas Aquinas, however, does not approve of tyrannicide, that he finds condemned by St. Paul's injunction to obey the authorities (Rom. 13, 1-7). The people should submit even to a tyrant. In order to avoid tyranny great care must be taken in the choice of kings, and the royal authority must not be absolute[8]. A good king will not exercise his office to obtain honor and glory (ch. 7), but only in view of a divine reward in heaven (ch. 8-9), a reward that tyrants will not receive (ch. 10; 12). He will realize that all the faithful are themselves kings and priests (*reges et sacerdotes*), for they participate in the royal priesthood (*regale sacerdotium*) of Christ, and that the supervision of this royal priesthood is not entrusted to kings, but to spiritual rulers, "priests, and principally the supreme pontiff, successor of Peter and vicar of Christ" (ch. 14).

In Book Two Thomas turns to the tasks that are proper to a king. The chief of these, and the only one that is considered in what Thomas himself wrote, is the building of cities. The location should be carefully selected, so that the climate will be moderate, the people will breathe pure air, have pure and sufficient water, and enough food available, preferably through agriculture, though commerce should be foreseen where it will be needed (II ch. 2-3). Aquinas recommends that most citizens live outside the walls of the city, in the countryside where they will work the land (II ch. 4). The rather surprising reason for this is that dissent comes frequently where many people congregate. In other words, Thomas Aquinas's ideal kingdom would be made of small towns, most citizens living in farms not far from them. In any case the people should live in an area that can be called *amoena*, that is, peaceful, tranquil, and agreeable, in which they will escape the extremes of misery and of excessive and irrational pleasure (*delicia*). In a word, the purpose of good government is that all may live according to the requirements of virtue[9].

One may presume that the king of Cyprus did not find this dissertation very practical, if indeed he was looking for support in a struggle with some of his more powerful subjects. That Thomas Aquinas composed it is nevertheless a valuable indication of the political mood of a period when sociology did not exist, democracy was not recommended, and the chief sources of political science were the doctrines of God and of creation, biblical and ancient history, the political writings of Plato and Aristotle, and the observation of nature.

*

The approach to political science was not essentially different in the works of Bonaventure, though the two scholastics are at variance on a major point. Bonaventure started from the principle that wisdom and justice are closely related. The task of a king is to guarantee civil justice, and so to pave the way for divine justice in the life of his subjects. Kingship, however, is naturally prone to become tyranny, for a king is caught by his functions between the attraction of wisdom, "which is from above," and the pull of "another, which is from below[10]." This latter leads to seek earthly wealth and pleasures. It is "earthly" and "animalistic." When it also leads to "the ambition of secular pomps" it becomes diabolical. "For pride is the root of all evils, and it is principally condemned in a diabolical king." One wonders if Bonaventure had a specific person in mind when he spoke of a diabolical king. In any case his judgment on monarchic government is illustrated by another passage, where he discussed "the form of the common life (*forma convivendi*)[11], and "the norm of presidence (*norma presidendi*), that is, how a prince must behave toward the people, and conversely[12]." Briefly, the people must "assist the one who punishes and vindicates. The Prince must not seek his own fortune (*utilitatem*) but that of the commonweal (*reipublicae*)." In the following lines, however, Bonaventure adopted a radical stance at a time when all the monarchies of Western Europe were hereditary:

> Today there is a great abomination among those who rule, for no captain is placed in a ship unless he knows the art of steering: How then is one who does not know how to rule placed in the commonweal? Hence, when they preside by virtue of succession, the commonweal is badly ruled.

This criticism of dynastic heredity implied a disapproval of the system that was in place in Christendom, with the major exception of the Holy Empire itself, where the emperor was chosen by a small group of hereditary electors. Kings and lower princes commonly acceded to power by heredity, which did not go without provoking a few wars of succession. While the kingdom of France was happily free of such struggles, Bonaventure's misgivings about the hereditary principle may well have arisen from his disappointment, when he sojourned in Paris to deliver his *Lectures on the Ten Commandments*, with the political shortcomings of king Louis's successor, his son Philippe III *le Hardi*.

*

Political concerns are inseparable from religious attitudes. Bishops and theologians hoped that Christian kings would pray the Holy Spirit to grant them the gift of wisdom, which should prevent them from falling into the false wisdoms that Bonaventure called "animal," focused on the belly, or "diabolical," aiming at self-glorification, or merely "earthly[13]," modeled on merely human concerns and principles. True wisdom is the exact opposite. It was revealed on the Cross, where Christ "taught contempt for the world's wisdom; and as he ascended to heaven he taught that one should desire God's wisdom and love the Fountain of life[14]." Divine wisdom is "a light (*lux*) that descends from God to the intellect, from the intellect to the affections (*affectus*), and as far as the lowest action[15]." This triple descent of wisdom "builds the church and the soul so that they become the dwelling place and the house of God, a house that is, I say, agreeable, beautiful, and solid[16]," built as it is on the seven columns that are as many steps leading up to wisdom. Both church and soul, however, are influenced by their societal environment. And this environment, at the time, was inseparable from the Jewish presence in Christendom. The relation between Christians and Jews formed a backdrop to all theological debates.

Located at another stratum of medieval society and in a different theological horizon, Jews dwelt in the Christian kingdoms as more or less unwanted strangers. They were treated basically as heretics, in keeping with the anti-Jewish measures of Lateran Council IV. In the predominantly Christian society Judaism stood out as a sociological and religious exception, unable to conform to the standards of the majority. Jews remained a people apart, who, as a whole, whatever the number of individual converts, did not recognize Jesus as the announced Messiah. No attention was paid by Christians to the providential aspect of the reconstruction of Judaism after the destruction of Jerusalem. Though mostly unsystematic, critical remarks occurred often enough in literature, in theology, and in reflections on law, for various forms of anti-Judaism to be constitutive part of the cultural horizon. The Jewish question was itself not foreign to the Joachimite expectation of a world-shaking event. As he based his argumentation on the Old Testament Joachim acknowledged the input of a former rabbi, converted to Christianity, Moses Sefardi, who as a Christian called himself Petrus Alphonsi[17]. In fact some of Joachim's drawings were borrowed from Alphonsi, notably the figuration of the Three Persons as interlocking circles. Joachim also composed a tractate with the purpose of converting Jews, that will retain our attention further on.

*

Analysis of the law provided a privileged vantage point from which to look at Judaism theologically. The Mosaic Law, revealed on Mount

Sinai (Ex. 19-31), still outlined the Hebrews' way of life, enshrined in the dietary and moral system of Leviticus, if not also, given the destruction of the Temple and the diaspora situation, in cultic practice. To what extent Jewish converts to Christianity were bound to the Law had been a controversial question since the argument between Paul and Peter in Antioch (Gal. 2,11-14). It was discussed in early Christian theology, as the Church Fathers attempted to determine the amount of Law that had been abolished because it was incompatible with the belief in the resurrection of Jesus[18]. While the general consensus settled on the principle that the Decalogue is valid for all times and cannot be abolished, interpretations of it varied, as in the Manichean doctrines regarding matter, the flesh, and sexuality, with which St. Augustine struggled on the way to his conversion. Medieval sectarian movements not infrequently declared some of the commandments obsolete. This may have been the case in the fifth century with Priscillian, who was accused of immorality and heresy[19], and beheaded in 385. In the thirteenth centuries the Cathars' dualistic tenets suggested various forms of immorality to their enemies, and all the more so as they denied that marriage was truly a sacrament, and as their solemn consecration to purity of doctrine and mores, the *consolamentum*, included a renunciation to all forms of sexuality[20]. Whether against heretics, Jews, or Muslims, however, accusations of immorality should not be taken literally. Since the first centuries of Christianity they had been part of the standard rhetoric of denigration for those who for whatever reasons did not fit the mold of orthodoxy. This had a remote origin in the Bible itself, where the prophets equated the worship of foreign gods with adultery and fornication[21].

Since the geographic parameters of the Church were identical with the Christian nations, the continuing presence of Jews embodied the oldest fault-line between orthodoxy and heterodoxy. The critique of Judaism on theological or moral grounds was therefore politically easy. Few were the emperors, kings, or lesser lords who trusted the Jewry in their lands. Many of them looked for opportunities to enrich themselves at the expense of Jews. Innocent III and Council IV of the Lateran had promulgated four anti-Jewish constitutions. Constitution 67 urged the authorities to protect their subjects from usury rates for which Jewish moneylenders were, rightly or wrongly, blamed[22]. Constitution 68 decreed that Jews in Christian lands must wear distinctive habits. Constitution 69 forbade them to be entrusted with public functions. Constitution 70 specified that converts from Judaism must give up the customary rituals of Jewish home life.

Although several pontifical decrees forbade violence against Jews, baptism under duress was not unheard of. The practice had even received a place of honor in the *Chanson de Roland*, an anonymous epic poem composed before 1066 to the glory of Charlemagne. When the great emperor conquered Saragossa, the Jews and Muslims of the city were given the choice of baptism or death:

> The Emperor has taken Saragossa.
> A thousand Frenchmen search the city,
> The synagogues and the mosques...
> No sorcery or falsity will remain...
> The King believes in God, wants to serve Him,
> His bishops bless the waters,
> Lead pagans to the baptistery.
> If anyone contradicts Charles
> He has him arrested, burned, or slain.
> Well over a thousand are baptized[23]...

Not only did secular lords see it as their duty to restrict the activities of Jews. One of the great mystics of the thirteenth century, Mechtild of Magdeburg (c.1208-c.1296), claimed that God himself had taught her "how Christians should behave towards Jews. They must pay them no honor. They must not live with them or pass the night with them. They must buy from them and sell to them without indulging in friendly company and without false cupidity[24]." In other words, Jews should be treated fairly in business, but Christians may not indulge in friendship or familiarity with them. Christian girls and women must not work as servants in Jewish households.

The Jews showed a totally admirable resilience before such measures. In their own circles they remained relatively free to study the Talmudic traditions, except when the secular arm obeyed papal injunctions to collect and burn the books of the Talmud. Rabbis took part, most often reluctantly, in public debates with bishops and theologians. A few were occasionally consulted by the handful of Christian scholars who studied Hebrew.

In these circumstances the refutation of Jewish doctrines was a tool to confirm Christian believers in their faith and eventually to convert Jews, a conversion that was considered all the more urgent as the *eschaton* was thought to be approaching. Fear of the coming end was fed by the multiplication of wars (the Crusades) and of false doctrines, such as could be seen in Gherardo's claims about Francis of Assisi, in the polemic of Guillaume de Saint-Amour against the friars, as also in the "Latin Averroism" that shook the university of Paris in the late 1260's.

*

Joachim's own writing on Jews is in the form of exhortation: *Exhortatio judoeorum*[25]. His interest in the Eternal Gospel was tied in a psychological knot made of many trends and dimensions. He was eager to convert the Jews to the Christian faith when there was still time, that is, before the door to the Kingdom was closed with the revelation of the Spirit. A firm believer in God's mercy, he was convinced that the revelation of the Eternal Gospel would be preceded by a time of favor for Jews, an invitation to them to recognize the Christ: "I sense that the time of mercy for them is at hand, the time of their consolation and conversion[26]." He focused attention on the basic truths that Jews do not accept, namely the doctrines of the Trinity, of the Incarnation, and, "what is no less dangerous, the spiritual understanding (of the Scriptures), as they affirm the letter that kills[27]." The Trinity and the Incarnation come from the tradition. The third point, however, no less important to Joachim than the first two, came from his own insight. Although *mysticus intellectus* has been "onerous" to Jews, because "until now it has been a portent of evil," it should no longer be so "where it shows that the time of your consolation is near."[28] In other words, the *concordia* that has been revealed to the abbot of Fiore brings the good news of the conversion of Jews.

Rather than directly refute Jewish objections to the Christian faith, Joachim explained that three essential points that he saw as the core of Christianity were already in the Old Testament. Indeed, Jews and

Christians are one in relation to the Father: "That the one we call Father is true Lord and true God is the common faith of you and us, and the one confession of both of us." The Jews, however, did not see that "the Angel of God" of the Bible is really God's eternal Son; and when he became incarnate they killed him. "From this killing it followed that the people of Israel are not his people, for they denied him in front of Pilate, when they said, 'We have no king but Caesar'[29]."

In the same way the Jews did not understand the "allegorical meaning" of the Old Testament: Elijah should be understood as John, the daughter of Sion as the Church, the people of Israel as the Christian people, Juda as "the confessors of the truth[30]." Given their difficulty in this regard Joachim at this point argued strictly, he declared, *secundum litteram*, "according to the letter," where the concord of the two Testaments is evident. At the same time, however, the enthusiastic abbot went beyond exegesis and entered the realm of prophecy, for he compared himself openly with Moses:

> And now, *o viri Judei*, hear my voice today and do not harden your hearts; hear also the voice of Moses announcing and saying the same from the mouth of almighty God, as I do today[31]...

Implicitly Joachim compared himself also with Peter, who, in the Acts of the Apostles 3, 12, had addressed the people of the Jews in a similar way, since in the Latin Vulgate that was the standard text of the Bible Peter began by addressing the Jews: *Viri israelitici*... Joachim's address, *o viri Judei*, is clearly reminiscent of Peter's speech. As Moses testified to the gospel of the Father, and Peter to the gospel of the Son made flesh, so Joachim testified to the *concordia* revealed to him by the Holy Spirit, that was, he believed, the key to the Scriptures. He wished the Jews to grasp "something of the concord of the two Testaments[32]." When this is achieved the Jews should received baptism, without which they cannot be worthy to enter into possession of the promises made to the seed of Abraham. Through "the water of holy baptism" they will receive the gift of the Holy Spirit, for "we believe that the invisible water descending from above is the word of God, which, as it reaches the element, makes the sacrament[33]." Then indeed the Christian hope will be fulfilled, "that we be both together, in our and your Christ, one priesthood and one kingdom."

*

Tractates about the Law presented a congenial context for discussion of Judaism, even though Judaism was no longer simply the old biblical religion, affected as it was by Talmudic traditions and the speculations of the Kabbalah. To what extent the laws of the Old Testament are relevant to Christians had been discussed already in patristic times. After Robert Grosseteste other authors composed more aggressive tractates *contra judaeos*, with the purpose of dispelling whatever doubts about the Christian faith the continuing presence of Jews could inspire among the faithful. Peter Damian (1007-1072) had written an *Antilogus contra judaeos*. Guibert de Tournai (d.1288) would later write a *Disputatio ecclesiae et synagogae*. Even if most of these texts were destined to be read by Christians rather than Jews, and they were generally not intended to fan hostility, they contributed to the precarious situation of Jews in Christian lands, not least through the hint that only people in bad faith could withstand their powerful argumentation. Although these works were occasionally cast in the form of a disputation between a priest and a rabbi, Jews and Christians did not hold friendly intellectual debates on an equal basis. When public disputations did take place, the rabbis were usually forced to attend by civil authorities. On the whole there was no friendly atmosphere in which Jews could explain their teachings to Christian thinkers, few of whom, in any case, cared enough to talk to them. Meanwhile, it was not uncommon for kings and princes to wonder if they ought to expel Jews from their territories. Several did so, seldom with total success. A decree expelling Jews from France had been promulgated in 1182 by king Philippe II Augustus, though it was not systematically enforced[34].

Given this pervasive anti-Judaism it was all too easy to justify moves against Jews with the argument that, as Bonaventure formulated it in a perspective that conflated the figures of Abel the just and of Jesus, "Christ was slain by his brothers, and a mark was placed on the Jews so that they should not be killed but be wanderers and refugees on the earth[35]." If this did not directly encourage the bloody pogroms that accompanied the crusades, it did not discourage temporal lords from exploiting Jews or keeping them on the move. Even Louis IX of

France is reported to have said: "I tell you that no one, unless he be a very good scholar, should debate with those people; a layman, when he hears the Christian faith gainsaid, should defend it only with the sword, which he should push into the belly as far as it can go[36]."

The situation of Jews was also Thomas Aquinas's concern. He composed the *Summa contra gentes* (from 1258 to 1263) to help preachers and missionaries who faced Jews and Muslims. He had previously been consulted by Alix de Bourgogne, duchess of Brabant (d. 1273), regarding the proper way to deal with Jews in her territories. In the short opusculum he composed for her, *De regimine judaeorum*[37], Thomas endorsed what was then the common view: "Rightly, by their own fault, Jews are or should be bound to perpetual servitude; and thus a prince may treat their goods as his own." He advocated moderation in the use of this principle, so that Jews would not lose all means of support. He did not explain, however, why the natural law that allows human beings to own what they need for living did not apply to Jews who lived among Christians.

A collection of Sunday sermons that Bonaventure preached in 1267/1268 illustrates what a serious and moderate thinker wished the Christian laity to know. On the Second Sunday of Advent, 1267, the people were told that St. Paul in Eph. 2:17 called the Jews "those who are near" because they had received the Law and the promise[38]. For the Third Sunday, however, the Jews' disregard of Jesus was blamed on ignorance, sophistic argumentation, and hatred of fraternity. The first of these three defects came from "the blindness of their malignity... Therefore they refused to avoid the evil of guilt or do the good of justice, for no one can be guided without the light of faith. Instead, they walk in darkness, seeking the falsehood of infidelity[39]." The second originated in misuse of knowledge and in the numerous errors that are nurtured by "debilitating cupidity,... distorting animal lust, and... inflating pride[40]." Finally, when Christ spoke the truth of life to them, "the Jewish people rejected heavenly grace." For this reason "they are said to hate their brother Christ and to be in darkness. Moreover they even called the good, evil, and the light, darkness... Therefore they walk in darkness and do not know where they go." On the nineteenth Sunday after Pentecost the Jews were called "assassins." God's wrath was given as the reason why, under the emperors Titus and Vespasian, "Jerusalem was completely destroyed and the Jews were killed, dispersed, and sold, thirty for one *denarium*, as they sold Christ for thirty *denarii*[41]." Thus, even a theologian who did not author an *Adversus judaeos* shared the distrust and hostility that characterized most of the church of his time.

The pattern of anti-Judaism appears clearly in Bonaventure's *Lectures on the Ten Commandments*, the first of the three series of lectures in which the Seraphic Doctor refuted Joachimite doctrines. On the one hand, Jews should not be blamed for behavior of which they are not guilty. Since the first three commandments forbid idolatry, pacts with the devil, "all the false and superstitious inventions of error,... and perverse appreciations of creaturely natures," Jews do not dabble with magic. A certain individual who attempted to become rich with the devil's help is said to have "sought for a magician among Jews and Christians, and he did not find one[42]..." On the other hand, crude objections to Christian belief, that are allegedly based on the first commandment, need to be refuted: "Jews sometimes insult us, and say that we do not well follow this commandment, and accuse us of transgressing it[43]," specifically because we affirm the divine Trinity, fill churches with pictures, and, as some Jews put it, adore a piece of bread. The refutation is ruled by a broad principle: "We Christians should see further than the Jewish people to whom these commandments were given[44]." The key to this wider perspective is the belief that Christ, the Word made flesh, is the Center of the universe.

As to the doctrine of the Trinity, "a certain Jew" jeers: "You say that God has a Son; why do you not give him a wife[45]?" This is a crass understanding (*vilissime*) of the Trinity that ought to be corrected by a brief statement of the true doctrine. This doctrine, however, cannot be grasped unless one "entertains the highest thoughts, not earthly thoughts; otherwise one cannot understand the high things of God (*altissima de Deo*). For when we posit the Trinity we do not posit Christ as a mere man, but as God with man." In order to see further than Jews one needs to think of God at a higher level than they commonly do. This is precisely Christian theology: to think about God "most highly and piously, most highly and truly, most highly and excellently" (*altissime et piissime, altissime et verissime, altissime et optime*[46]).

That churches are filled with pictures could not be denied. It was a common practice, not only to place statues in churches and to use the windows to illustrate the lives of saints, but also to cover the walls with paintings and symbols of the revelation and the heavenly world. The traditional pattern, inherited from early Romanesque art, showed scenes from the Old Testament at the lowest level, from the New Testament higher up, and from the Apocalypse of John at the highest level. While "sculptures of the divinity" are not tolerated, adoration (*adoratio duliae*) is proper before the images of Christ "by reason of the One who is signified[47]."

The third accusation belittles the eucharist. Bonaventure attributed this to the low level of Jewish thoughts and concerns: "The Jew errs by thinking in an earthly way[48]." A pedestrian method of reading Scripture and construing doctrine can only lead to error.

*

Judaism was not simply a foil for Christian faith and belief. Its very permanence in spite of the social stigma that was attached to it acted also as a critique of the shortcomings of most Christians. Largely for this reason Judaism remained a recurrent theme in Bonaventure's *Lectures on the Six Days*, where a dozen passages evoke it[49]. The very first of these lectures opens on an unexpected piece of anti-Judaism:

> Whom should one address? The Church, for the holy must not be given to dogs and pearls thrown before pigs... One should address the Church, the gathering of those who are rational; the synagogue is an assembly of animals and men who live like beasts (*brutaliter*)[50].

This pejorative symbolism may have been suggested by a controversy about the Talmud that broke out in Paris in 1240. The affair was extremely involved. Gregory IX (pope, 1227-1241) was generally overzealous in imposing restrictions on the Jews in Christian lands[51]. He was heavily influenced in this by a convert from Judaism, Nicholas Donin, who, like many among the Talmudic scholars who became Christian, was particularly zealous in arguing with his former colleagues. Donin sent the pope a list of thirty-five articles, with citations from the Talmud, which, he claimed, revealed the anti-Christian orientation of the Jewish writings. On 6 September 1239 Gregory therefore urged the bishops of France, England, and Castille to "seize and burn all the Jewish books that could be found[52]." Again on 12 September he wrote to the bishop of Paris, to the prior of the Dominicans, and to the provincial of the Franciscans in the French capital, to make sure that the secular arm order Jews to surrender their copies of the Talmud. These books must then be destroyed by fire, for the Talmud, the pope asserted, "is known to us as the chief instrument of Jewish unbelief."

This was not only an anti-Jewish measure. It was part of the pope's struggle with Frederick II (1194-1250, emperor in 1212), who considered himself the king of the three religions, Judaism, Christianity, and Islam. Although he fought in the Sixth Crusade and proclaimed himself King of Jerusalem, Frederick openly consorted with Muslim princes, and he had great admiration for Islam. He also protected Jews. In spite of what the popes expected from Christian princes, he showed no inclination to favor Christianity over the other monotheistic religions. Moreover, his ambitions regarding Southern Italy ran against the politics of all the popes of his time. The emperor in fact was a major topic of discussion at the First General Council of Lyon (28 June, 5 to 17 July 1245), over which Innocent IV (1243-1254) had presided in person. The Council's decision to depose the emperor[53] remained without any further effect than exasperating Frederick, who continued to ignore Gregory's injunctions.

Although pope Gregory was on good terms with the king of France Louis IX, his instructions concerning Jews were not carried out in French lands. From his Spanish mother, Blanche de Castille (1185-1252), who served as the model of his kingship, Louis had inherited a profound piety, a great devotion to the church, an eagerness to do justice to all his subjects, and also a determination that could verge on abruptness. Instead of destroying Jewish books he ordered a public disputation between theologians and rabbis to discuss the nature of the Talmud. This took place in 1240. How many friars attended this event is not known. Accounts of the debate, however, must have reached professors and students in the theological schools. When therefore, a few years later, they lectured at the university of Paris, neither Thomas nor Bonaventure could ignore the question of Judaism as a post-Christian, and more or less anti-Christian, doctrine.

There was nevertheless an ambiguity in the Christian view of the synagogue. Any one who traveled to Strasbourg in the late 1260's could see the statuary of the South porch, done around 1225-1230, as a striking illustration of the belief that *synagoga* stands in opposition to *ecclesia*[54]. The faithful who enter the church through this porch pass between the statues of two women, *ecclesia* on the left, *synagoga* on the right. Synagogue, blindfolded, leaning on a broken staff, wears a simple vestment that could be a nightshirt. Church, in royal garments, crowned like a queen, stands in self-assurance. Which of the two, however, signifies the true faith? The Church triumphant can only be in heaven, where saints enjoy the vision of God in the light of glory. Here on earth it is only when, one's staff broken, bereft of human support, one has become blind to the pomp of the world and the devil, that it is possible, by grace, to walk in pure faith. Of such a faith the woman-synagogue of Strasbourg cathedral is really a better symbol than the woman-church. For the Church militant is not the New Jerusalem. Only to the extent that she is blind does she walk by faith, for she is then guided by a purely interior light, in keeping with the paradoxical biblical text, often quoted by Bonaventure, *Et nox illuminatio mea in deliciis meis* (Vulgate, Ps. 138, 11); "The night is my light in my delights." The two statues of Strasbourg, therefore, show the Church triumphant (*ecclesia*) and the Church militant (*synagoga*) better than the gatherings of Jews and of Christians[55].

The ambiguity of the image of the synagogue cannot be unrelated to the theologians' hesitation to praise the Jews, who, "at one time, so acknowledged the authority of the book of Job that they put it in the Ark, along with the rod and the tablets[56]." Their rejection of Jesus even had a respectable motivation, for they identified the coming of the Messiah with the gift of universal peace; and unfortunately "there still are quarrels and heresies. Hence the Jews, who hope in this [messianic peace], believe that the Christ has not yet come[57]." And they apply the relevant text of Isaiah (Is. 2, 4) to the first advent of Christ instead of the second. Moreover, those who rejected Jesus after the resurrection were overwhelmingly dazzled by the Sun-Christ, in keeping with the prophecy of Amos, 9, 8: "At noon the sun killed the

Jews." So it was that when Christ "was at his greatest power, namely after the resurrection and the ascension, the Jews were blinded[58]." In any case it is certain, on the testimonies of Isaiah and Paul, that they will eventually be converted to Christ.

The contrast between the Jews of Jesus' s time and today's Christians does not always favor the latter: "The Jews did not want to hear the wisdom coming from the mouth of Wisdom; but we have Christ within us and we do not want to hear his wisdom[59]." The first to believe in Jesus were in fact Jews. Parallel to the two periods of the Old Testament, before the Law and after the Law, there are two periods of the New Testament, "the time of the call to the Gentiles, and the time of the call to the Jews, which will be at the end[60]." When the two sons of Juda were born (Gen. 38,27-30), Zara first pushed his hand out and the midwife tied a scarlet thread to it, but he then withdrew his hand. Phares was therefore born first, breaking the wall. Thus the Jews believed first, and then they withdrew their hand. When all the Gentiles are Christian, Zara will come out and the Jewish people will be converted.

The theologians did not forget the contribution of Jews to the primitive church. "This church, which began among Jews,—for 'at one time three thousand were converted, at another time six thousand' (Acts 2: 44),—had the tree of life, faith, since 'my just one lives from faith;' it also had the tree of knowledge, the Law[61]..." The extent to which the Law was binding for Christians, however, had to be debated. And this was where many Jews who had recognized the Messiah went astray, misled by an excessive zeal for Torah:

> ...bending over the Law like lovers over their wife, they ate of the tree of knowledge in order to keep the Law, and they assented to the snake who persuaded them to keep the Law, and hence the Ebionites' heresy was born, —that the Law must be kept along with the Gospel—; and zeal for the Law was such that Peter consented to that pretense, but God's grace saved him.—And their ejection followed when God withdrew from them; they were dispersed and cursed in their work, and devoured as it were by two bears, Titus and Vespasian. And thus Cain, killer of his brother, namely, the people of the Jews, received the mark[62].

The life of faith is itself not unlike the march of the Hebrews in the wilderness. The disciples should not tire of the heavenly manna. They should not "be carnal like the sons of Israel, who found only one taste [in manna], while others, spiritual persons, found the suavity of every savor[63]." Who are those spiritual persons? In an image that would not have been rejected by the rabbis, the meditation of Scripture through the gift of intellect is likened to the chewing of cud by animals with two stomachs:

> Rumination is a repeated recall to taste of food that has been in the stomach. The sweet discourses of Scripture are always to be ruminated for their savor by the eager soul's application. A maidservant's embraces are not to be preferred to those of a bride, or the food of pigs to the bread of children, or the acorns from which Absalom hangs to the fruits that refresh with spiritual strength[64]...

The meaning is evidently that the true Christian must be a contemplative. By implication, the true church is the Bride, not the maidservant. The kiss for which she longs, as St. Bernard had preached in his sermons on the Song of Songs, is the kiss of the mouth (Cant. 1, 1), which, in the present life, can only be received in the total darkness of the night of faith.

The later Franciscan Nicholas de Lyra (c. 1270-1349) frequently quoted the biblical commentaries of a well-known rabbi, Rashi[65] (1030-1105). The great scholastics, however, did not know Hebrew well enough to consult Jewish writings directly. It was nonetheless one of the ironies of the papal campaign against the Talmud that the thirteenth century was itself a flourishing period for mystical Judaism. This was true in Spain, in the Rhineland, and in Southern France West of the Rhone river, notably in the cities of Narbonne and Lunel. Now, in 1260 Bonaventure presided over a general chapter of the Franciscans in Narbonne. Though no direct line is traceable from the one to the other, there is an intriguing analogy between his conception of the Word of God and a theory that had been advanced a few decades earlier by a Jewish scholar and mystic of the Narbonne area, Isaac the Blind[66] (d. c.1235): All human language derives from the four letters of the tetragrammaton, the Name of God—*HaShem*,—that is too holy to be pronounced. And the Franciscan interpretation of

Augustine's doctrine of illumination viewed the Word of God, eternally spoken by the Father, as indeed the Center of all. It is a "ray of truth" from the divine Word that enables humans to speak and communicate by illuminating the "truth of words" (*veritas vocum*) in their mind[67].

*

Theological reflection in the thirteenth century took place on a backdrop of anti-Judaism, the result of the uneasy coexistence of Christians and Jews in Western society. A standard criticism of Jews was that their biblical exegesis remained excessively literal, as could even be illustrated by the speculations of the Kabbalah, where it was not unusual to consider every letter of the Hebrew Bible inspired. This gave the Kabbalists an unexpected kinship with Joachim, who started his speculations only after ascertaining to his satisfaction that the entire course of the Church's history was prefigured in the letter of the Old Testament.

Reflection on the Law drew attention to the concept of Torah that was still at the heart of Jewish religion. The letters of Paul, that of James, and the four Gospels underlined its importance at the origins of Christianity, even when the first Christians, following Paul, took their distance from the Pharisaic Judaism that survived the destruction of the Holy City by "two bears, Titus and Vespasian." Seen from a Christian standpoint, Judaism survived the death of the Messiah, but it did not experience the resurrection. It still hoped in the coming of the messianic times, and it kept the Law as best it could without the Temple. Jews have thus walked by faith through the centuries, carrying on their shoulders and feeling in their flesh the weight of disapproval that Christians did not hide from them.

Notes

1 Louis returned from the crusade in 1254; it had been a series of military disasters and had cost a fortune, the king having paid a heavy ransom after he was captured in Egypt.

2 Philippe III's chief adviser, Pierre de la Brosse, had been his father's barber. Widowed in 1271 from Isabelle d'Aragon, Philippe III remarried Marie de Brabant in 1274, who was soon in deadly conflict with de la Brosse. This led to a plot against the queen and to Pierre de la Brosse's death for high treason in 1278.

3 To keep the kingdom of Sicily Charles d'Anjou fought Manfred, who was killed at the battle of Benevento in 1266; he then fought and executed Conradin; he was in turn beaten by the Spaniard Pedro de Aragon, who took Sicily in 1282.

4 Sophie de Sède, *La Sainte Chapelle et la politique de la fin des temps*, Paris: Julliard, 1972, p.320-332.

5 After bk III, 6, the commentary was completed by Peter of Auvergne (d. 1304): Chenu, *Introduction à l'étude de saint Thomas d'Aquin*, Paris: Vrin, 1950, p. 191.

6 Chenu, *Introduction...*, p. 286-288.

7 *Hoc igitur officium rex suscepisse cognoscat, ut sit in regno sicut in corpore anima, et sicut Deus in mundo* (Pierre Mandonnet, *S. Thomae Aquinatis Opuscula Omnia*, vol. 1, Paris: Lethielleux, 1927, ch. 12, p. 352).

8 *Simul etiam sic temperetur potestas, ut in tyrannidem de facili declinare non possit* (ch. 6, p. 323).

9 *Finis quem rex in civitate sui regiminis debet intendere, est vivere secundum virtutem* (ch. 8, p. 360).

10 Bonaventure, *Collationes in septem donis Spiritus Sancti,* IX, 2 (*Obras de San Buenaventura,* vol. 5, 1958, Madrid: BAC, p. 584).

11 *In Hexaëmeron* V, 18 (*Obras,...*, p. 286).

12 *In Hexaëmeron* V, 19 (*Obras,...*, vol. 3, p. 286).

13 *In septem donis,* IX, 3 (*Obras*, vol. 5, p.586).

14 *In septem donis*, IX, 4 (*Obras*, p. 586).

15 *In septem donis...*, IX, 5 (*Obras*, p. 588).

16 *In septem donis...*, IX, 8 (*Obras*, p. 590).

17 A physician to Alphonsus VI of Leon and Castile, rabbi Moises Sefardi (1062-c.1140), born in Huesca, changed his name to Petrus Alphonsi (in honor of St Peter and king Alphonsus) when he was baptized in 1106; he wrote *Dialogi in quibus impiae judaeorum opiniones... confutantur* (PL 157, 535-672); see A. L. Williams, *Adversus Judaeos*, London: Cambridge University Press, 1935.

18 Tavard, "Christianity and Israel: Is the Church Schismatic?" (*Downside Review*, October 1955, p. 347-358).

[19] Henry Chadwick, *Priscillian of Avila*, Oxford: Clarendon Press, 1976.

[20] Stephen Runciman, *The Medieval Heretic. A Study of the Christian Dualist Heresy*, London: Cambridge University Press, 1955; those who had received the *consolamentum* were not called perfect, but *revêtus* (those who have been clothed), that is, whose sexuality is no longer visible.

[21] See the parable of the adulterous wife in Amos 3, 1-5.

[22] COD, p. 241-242; curiously enough, this constitution immediately follows another, on "the cupidity of clerics."

[23] Gerard J. Brault, *The Song of Roland. An Analytical Edition*, vol. 2: Oxford Text and English Translation, State College: Pennsylvania State University Press, 1978, p. 223-224; the translation has been slightly modified.

[24] Quoted in Emilie Zum Brunn and Georgette Epiney-Burgard, *Women Mystics in Medieval Europe*, St. Paul, MN: Paragon House, 1989, p. 194, note 22.

[25] Arsenio Frugoni, ed., *Adversus Judeos*, Rome: Istituto storico italiano, 1957; the title of Joachim's piece varies in the manuscripts; *exhortatio* is more appropriate to the tone and content of the work.

[26] *...adesse sentio tempus miserendi eis, tempus consolationis et conversionis eorum* (Frugoni..., p. 3).

[27] *...quod non est minoris periculi, spiritualem intellectum, statuentes litteram quae occidit.*

[28] *...licet onerosus sit vobis mysticus intellectus, pro eo quod hactenus nuntius mali fuit, hic tamen onerosus esse non debet, ubi vobis vicinum esse indicat tempus consolationis vestrae* (Frugoni, p. 26).

[29] Frugoni, p. 48.

[30] Frugoni, p. 86.

[31] *Et nunc, o viri Judei, audite hodie vocem meam, et nolite obdurare corda vestra, quinimmo audite vocem Moysi, eadem vobis que et ego hodie ex ore omnipotentis Dei annuntiantis et dicentis...* (Frugoni, p. 89); the text that is then quoted is Leviticus 26, 39-41.

[32] *...ut percipiatis aliquid de concordia duorum testamentorum* (Frugoni, p. 99).

[33] *Ipsa est enim hereditas que promissa est semini Abrae, ad cujus possessionm intrare non estis digni nisi prius perfundamini sacri unda baptismi ut, abluti a sorde infidelitatis vestrae, accipiatis ut vobis hic promittitur, donum Spiritus Sancti... credimus aquam invisibilem que descendit desuper esse verbum Dei, que cum accedit ad elementum, fit sacramentum* (Frugoni..., p. 92).

[34] When the Dominican pope Pius V (pope, 1566-1572) expelled Jews from the Papal States he excepted those who lived in Rome and in Ancona; see K. R. Stow, *Catholic Thought and Papal Jewish Policy*, New York: Jewish Theological Seminary, 1965.

[35] *In Hexaëmeron*, XIV, 18 (*Obras*, vol. 3, p. 440).

[36] Quoted in Marius Sepet, *Saint Louis*, Paris: Librairie Lecoffre, 1905, p. 76; the information comes from the *Mémoires* of Joinville, the king's chronicler.

[37] Heinz Schreckenburg, *Die christlichen Adversus-Judaeos-Texte und ihr literarisches und historisches Umfeld* (*13.-20. Jh.*), Frankfurt am Main: Peter Lang, 1994, p. 249-259.

[38] Guy Bougerol, ed., *Sancti Bonaventurae Sermones Dominicales*, Grottaferrata: Collegio San Bonaventura, 1977, p. 155.

[39] *Sermones…, sermo 4*, n. 13, p. 161.

[40] *Sermones…*, n. 13, p. 162.

[41] *Sermones…, sermo 46*, n. 10, p. 450.

[42] *De decem praeceptis*, II, 23 (*Obras,* vol. 5, p. 644).

[43] III, 8 (*Obras,* p. 656).

[44] *Nos christiani ultra illum judaicum populum, cui haec mandata fuerunt data, videre debemus* (II, 21: *Obras,* p. 642).

[45] III, 11 (*Obras*, p. 656).

[46] *In Hexaëmeron,* IX, 23 (*Obras,* vol. 3, p. 360).

[47] *In decem praeceptis*, III, 12 (*Obras,* vol. 5, p. 658).

[48] *In decem praeceptis*, III, 13 (*Obras*, vol. 5, p. 658).

[49] The Delorme edition contains fewer references to Judaism than the standard edition (I/I, 30; I/III, 35; III/III, 24-26, 35; III/IV, 3-6), but their language is no less forceful.

[50] *In Hexaëmeron,* I, 1-2 (*Obras*, vol. 3, p. 176-178).

[51] The list and analysis of his letters, bulls, and decrees against Jews takes more than twenty pages in Schreckenburg, *Die christlichen..,* p. 109-133.

[52] Schreckenburg, *Die christichen...*, p. 127-128.

[53] *Bulla depositionis,* in COD, p. 354-259.

[54] The cathedral was still in construction, the central aisle being finished only in 1274; the transept was older *(Dictionnaire des églises de France*, vol. 5, Paris: Lafont, p. 164).

[55] There was another ambiguity, of a linguistic nature, in the medieval references to Jews. The term *Judaei* can refer to the Hebrews of Mosaic times, to the contemporaries of Jesus, and to medieval Jews indifferently, as in the following citations:—(1) «The carnal and gluttonous Jews, as soon as they felt hungry, wished to be in the land of Egypt with pots of meats» (Bougerol, *Sermones..., sermo* 35, n. 9, p. 377).—(2) "The Jews believed that they had refuted Christ, and they shouted: If you are the Son of God come down from the Cross" (I, 28).—(3) «The Jews attribute to Solomon what is said of Christ in Psalm 44, 3" (III, 16). Such references remain general and often vague. Although some are not derogatory, many are openly hostile, as when they use the scriptural, yet insulting terms, «dogs» and «pigs,» or when they allude to those who had Jesus killed.

[56] *In Hexaëmeron*, XIV, 16 (*Obras*, vol. 3, p. 440).

[57] XV, 24 (*Obras*, vol. 3, p. 462).

[58] XIII, 26 (*Obras*, vol. 3, p. 422).

[59] II, 7 (*Obras*, vol. 3, p. 208).

[60] XVI, 4 (*Obras*, vol. 3, p. 470).

[61] XVI, 22 (*Obras*, 3, p. 482).

[62] XVI, 23 (*Obras*, 3, p. 482).

[63] XIX, 18 (*Obras* 3, p. 548); the reference is to Numb. 21, 5.

[64] *Delorme,* vision 3, coll. 7, n. 17-18, p. 218.

[65] Herman Hailpern, *Rashi and the Christian Scholars,* Pittsburgh: University of Pittsburgh Press, 1963, p. 105-110. Already in the twelfth century Hugh of St. Victor alluded to several of Rashi's interpretations in *Adnotationes elucidatoriae,* without naming him (PL. 175, 35-114).

[66] Gershom Scholem, *Kabbalah,* Jerusalem: Ketter Publishing House, 1974, p. 42-47; Isaac the Blind was the son of another notable mystic, Abraham ben David, the author of a "kabbalistic commentary on the thirteen attributes of God listed in Exodus 34, 6-7" (Georges Vajda, *L'Amour de Dieu dans la théologie juive du moyen âge,* Paris; Vrin, 1957, p. 6-7).

[67] IV, 18 (*Obras* 3, p. 266).

Chapter 4
The Protocol of Anagni

Shortly after Gherardo's Liber introductorius, with its surprising conception of the Eternal Gospel, hit the streets of Paris, pope Innocent IV was alerted by the bishop of Paris, Renaud Mignon de Corbeil (bishop, 1250-1268). Innocent, who, as we shall see in the next chapter, paid a willing ear to Guillaume de Saint-Amour, immediately ordered an inquiry into the doctrines of both Gherardo da Borgo San Donnino and the one whom Gherardo presented as his spiritual mentor, Joachim di Fiore. For this purpose he appointed a commission of three cardinals, Odo, bishop of Tusculum, Stephan, bishop of Praenestina (who did not attend in person, but sent a representative), and the well-known Dominican theologian, Hugh de Saint-Cher (d. 1263), cardinal-priest of Santa Sabina. As Innocent IV died before the commission had time to meet, it was Alexander IV who eventually received its report.

The commission met at Anagni, where pope Alexander was in residence. The commissioners were provided with a list of thirty-one errors that Guillaume de St-Amour accused Gherardo and Joachim of professing. In July 1255 they received the assistance of a Frenchman, Florentius or Florent (d.1266), bishop of St-Jean-d'Acre in Palestine, who brought with him lengthy excerpts from Joachim's writings. Since Florent turned out to be the sharpest critic of the founder of the Fiorensians, his name seems particularly ironic, and all the more so as at least one modern scholar, otherwise well informed, has taken the Latin version of his name, spelt here "Florensius," as designating the Order of Fiore: "Fiore," he writes, "supplied the writings of Joachim to the Commission of Anagni[1]..." Bishop Florent was in fact unconnected with the Fiorensians, and he turned out to be a determined adversary of Joachim's doctrines. In addition, the cardinals called on the expertise of a Dominican stationed in Anagni, who is simply called Peter in the Commission's report. For a reason that is not clear, they also got the help of a Byzantine bishop of the Patriarchate of Constantinople, Bonevaletus, bishop of Panedensis[2].

*

The Protocol is the name given to the report of the *ad hoc* pontifical commission. It devotes much more space to Joachim than to Gherardo, the friar being eliminated in three pages, out of forty-two in the whole document. The heart of Gherardo's doctrine is presented briefly: "The spirit of life left the two Testaments around the year 1200 to make room for the Eternal Gospel[3]." Gherardo claims that there are now in existence three "books of the Eternal Gospel," all composed by Joachim: the *Concordia*, the "New Apocalypse," and the "Ten-cord Psalter." Several analogies, that Gherardo cast in the form of trilogies, are cited in the Protocol. Among them: the Old Testament has a star-like clarity, the New is moonlike, the Eternal Gospel sunlike. Or also, the Scriptures have three parts,—old, new, eternal,—that correspond to the first, the second, and the third heaven. These three parts are distinct works of the Father, of the Son, and of the Spirit: "Another part has been given to us, at that time when the Holy Spirit works with the characteristic of mystery[4]." The Old Testament and the gospel of Christ are literal. The gospel of the Spirit alone is purely spiritual. Three states of the world correspond to the three gospels. After the time of fear and the law, and the time of faith, the time of the Spirit will be dominated by charity. Filled with grace, it will be "without obscurity and without images..., without the obscurities of the images of the two Testaments." The first Testament was heralded by Abraham, Isaac, and Jacob. The second was inaugurated by "Zachary, John the Baptist, and the man Christ Jesus[5]." The Eternal Testament in turn has been inaugurated by "a man in linen garments, an angel with a sharpened scythe, and another angel bearing the sign of the Living God." These three appeared around the year 1200. At least the first and the third are easily identifiable: Joachim bore the white Cistercian habit, and Francis was marked with the stigmata of the Lord, who appeared to him at Mount La Verna in the form of a crucified Seraph. As to the scythe-bearing angel, it must be Gherardo himself, the awakener, who pointed to the other two. Summing up its case, the Protocol declares

Gherardo's doctrines filled with "errors and stupidities[6]," and based entirely on the doctrines of Joachim.

*

The presentation and criticism of Joachim's ideas fill up six sections of the Protocol, which deal respectively with the foundation of the doctrine and with five specific items. The argumentation cites long passages from the writings of Joachim. The words of the abbot are left to speak for themselves, and the commentary is reduced to a minimum.

The foundation (*fundamentum*) is a distinction, imagined by Joachim, between three perfections (*status*) or successive periods (*tempora*) of the world, which however are not entirely successive since they dovetail into one another at the beginning and at the end of the second period. The time of the flesh, that began with Adam, bore fruit after Abraham for thirteen generations, and it ended with the coming of John the Baptist and Jesus Christ. The time between flesh and spirit, "initiated by the prophet Elijah," has born fruit, "through Christ, who is the true king and priest," until the present moment[7]. The time of the Spirit began "in the days of St. Benedict," and will bear fruit until the end of the world.

This threefold sequence suggests a correspondence between each period and one of the Three Persons, who are thus believed to act on earth successively rather than together, though the works of the Son and of the Spirit coincide in part. As there are the Father, the Son, and the Spirit in heaven, there are also three forms of life on earth, —married, clerical, and monastic,—that correspond to three Gospels or Testaments, Old, New, and Eternal. Joachim summed it up in a message he attributed to the Holy Spirit, who "speaks of the Son and of himself with action more than with the voice, and says: Until now the Son works with the Father, and I work[8]."

The five items that follow in the Protocol were believed by Joachim to be implied in the foundation. The first is developed in a long illustration[9], dotted with quotes, of Joachim's description of the three states of the world and of the Church. The second[10] is Joachim's "incredible exaltation of a certain order of monks," his denigration of the clerical state and his expectation of its disappearance "along with the active life in the Church[11]." This was illustrated by Joachim's opposition of Peter (the active and clerical life) and John (the contemplative and monastic life). The third point[12] is Joachim's announcement of "two antichrists, one of whom will come at the end of the second period, the other at the end of the third[13]." The fourth point[14] is Joachim's teaching "on the letter of the gospel, and on its author, the Lord Jesus Christ and the apostles, and on the sacraments[15]." The work of Christ lies at the level of the letter that kills, unless the Spirit gives it life. In itself it is only a *figura*, a sketch, that needs the further coming of the Spirit. Joachim's demonstration of this argues from (1) the distinction between the letter and the spirit[16], (2) the role of Jesus Christ as a "figure and similitude of One who is to come with his own at the beginning of the third period[17]," and, (3) Joachim's view of baptism: After the water, that is already available, the fire is still to come[18], and this fire is the Spirit.

The fifth and final point is Joachim's conception of the Holy Trinity[19]. The abbot attacked Peter Lombard no less than the heretics Sabellius and Arius. He distinguished between "one" (*unus*: the unity of one Person) and "oneness" (*unitas*: the unity of several who agree together). He held it wrong to say that "the Father and the Son and the Spirit are one." Rather one should say: the Three are "one God," for "neither trinity nor unity can be said of one Person." On the contrary, "Trinity is said of the Three Persons; Unity is said of the substance, not of one Person, but of the Three Persons[20]." The divine Persons are like the tribes of Judah, Benjamin, and Levi: together they constitute one people, and none of them is the whole people.

Since Joachim illustrated his teachings with drawings and diagrams, the Protocol examines the central figuration. The Son and the Spirit would be like two sharp angles at the bottom of what should be a triangle, while the Father, at the top, is an obtuse angle or rather two angles[21]. Such an image in reality abolishes the equality of the Persons, and leaves the Father in "obscurity or confusion" (*obtusio seu hebetudo figurae*[22]). But, as the Protocol argues, this evidently contradicts the utter simplicity of the first and eternal Principle; and it is contradicted by "all philosophy." In the Incarnation, "the Son received the human nature in the unity of his Person." Likewise, according to Joachim, "the

Spirit received the form of a dove as the image (*figura*) of Holy Mother Church[23]." Although the point is not emphasized in the Protocol, such an image suggests that Joachim's errors extend to the Incarnation of the divine Word and to the mission of the Holy Spirit.

To sum up, the Protocol of Anagni declared Joachim a heretic with a clarity that is proportional to the admirable succinctness of its comments. It supported the decree of Lateran Council IV. It also went much further. Not only was Joachim's critique of the Lombard declared mistaken. Not only were his prophecies of a new coming of the Spirit, of a new monastic order, and of a dawning third *status* of the Church denounced as being entirely false. His understanding of the Three Persons and of their unity was itself judged to be completely erroneous. The Protocol of Anagni was as thorough in its examination of the Joachimite writings as it was critical of Joachim as a thinker and a prophet.

*

After taking cognizance of the report of the commission, pope Alexander took his time reaching his own conclusion. His decision was issued more than a year later, in October 1255. Alexander fully agreed with the commissioners' judgement on Gherardo da Borgo San Donnino. He did not, however, endorse their negative conclusions regarding Joachim. The bull *Libellum quemdam*, that the pope addressed to the bishop of Paris on 23 October 1255, ordered Gherardo's *Liber introductorius* to be destroyed. Explicitly Gherardo was a heretic. Unbending, but never relapse since he never renounced his erroneous doctrines, he was not even tried by the Inquisition, and he spent the rest of his life in Franciscan friaries in his homeland of Sicily. Meanwhile, Giovanni da Parma (1209-1289), the Master general who had protected Gherardo without openly supporting his theology, was forced to resign at the general chapter of the *Ara coeli* in 1257, presumably under pressure from the pope. His resignation opened the way to the election of Bonaventure as his successor.

Since the *Liber introductorius* included the text of "the first book of the Eternal Gospel"—Joachim's *Concordia*,—the sentence to burn the book could be taken to imply a condemnation of the *Concordia*.

Explicitly, however, Alexander's decree kept silent about Joachim, his works, his theology, and his prophecies. Officially no shadows were cast by the pope on the memory of the Calabrian abbot and prophet, whose official standing remained what it was at the end of the Fourth Lateran Council. As a theologian he had simply misunderstood Peter Lombard. Whatever he may have thought privately,— and he nowhere indicated explicitly that he disapproved of the conclusions of the Protocol,—Alexander did not condemn Joachim or his doctrines.

Why this difference of treatment for the two authors who were equally denounced as heretics in the Protocol of Anagni? The reason the pope gives is simple, too simple: Joachim was a good Catholic. But since this was, precisely, the question, it could not be the premise of the argument. If the pope's reasoning, however, cannot be reconstructed with certainty, one can discern some of its facets. On the one hand, Alexander's lenience toward Joachim had a precedent in the judgment of his predecessor Honorius III, who had declared on 17 December 1220 (bull *Ex parte dilectorum*): "We recognize him to be a Catholic person, and the regular observance that he instituted salutary[24]." Furthermore, in a letter to the bishops of Cosenza and of Bisignano, Honorius had ordered them to

> make public, in defense of the monks of the Order of Fiore, that abbot Joachim was not a heretic,... but he ordered all his writings to be sent to the Pontiff to be approved or even corrected by apostolic judgment, and he professed to hold that faith which the Roman Church holds[25].

There was a certain amount of naïveté in pope Honorius's trust that Joachim was a good and orthodox Catholic simply because he had written that he wanted his brother abbots to present his works to the Holy See and abide by any ensuing judgment concerning their orthodoxy. Firstly, it should have been natural to be suspicious of the fact that Joachim had not himself sent all his writings to Rome and to wonder why he left this task to others. Why wait for a posthumous examination of his doctrines, if he was willing to correct them? Admittedly, in his letter of the year 2000 to the Fiorensian abbots, Joachim had blamed the turmoil of the period for his failure to apply to Rome: "Because" he wrote, "of the anguish of the times I have not been able until now to present these opuscula to the Apostolic Summit[26]..." Surely, however, the troubles were not such that no correspondence was possible between Calabria and the city of Rome, or wherever in central Italy the pope elected to reside. Neither Honorius nor Alexander, however, seem to have paid any attention to the real circumstances that Joachim's letter of 2000 was occulting. One can of course argue in Alexander's defense that it was right for him to respect the judgment of his predecessor. In the case of Innocent IV's decrees that favored the secular clergy over the Friars, however, Alexander did not hesitate to adopt the opposite position and to restore the Friars to their previous privileges. Respect for the views expressed by a recent bishop of Rome could therefore not have occupied a prominent place in his reasoning.

On the other hand, pope Alexander was confronted at the same moment with the virulent onslaught of Guillaume de St-Amour on the Mendicants. Alexander was caught between the horns of a dilemma. On one side, Gherardo da Borgo San Donnino and his reading of Joachim threatened the peace of the Church with false prophecies that a number of Franciscans were taking as the truth. On the other side, the archenemy of the friars, Guillaume de St-Amour, also threatened the peace of the Church. His explicit critique of the friars implied an implicit critique of the popes and bishops who, as Guillaume saw it, had imposed these new teachers upon the university. In these circumstances the pope's compromise may have been, in the short run, prudent.

Alexander IV unequivocally condemned the most extreme positions. Gherardo and his doctrines were denounced in *Libellum quemdam*. Guillaume's strictures against evangelical poverty were rejected in a largely redundant series of documents: *Veri solis* (17 October 1256), addressed to the king of France, *Non sine multa* (19 October 1256), to the bishops of France and Burgundy, *Quidam scripturae* (21 October 1256) to the bishops of Tours, Rouen, Paris, and other cities. Respecting the memory of Joachim could have a certain advantage in Southern Italy, where the Order of Fiore was still flourishing. Given the evidence of Joachim's writings it seems doubtful that pope Alexander really thought that the Calabrian prophet was fully orthodox. In any case he could hardly foresee the persistence of Joachimite ideas in diverse forms, in and outside the Church. Whether it was due to a failure of nerve or to a failure of judgment, Alexander IV's divided decision turned out to be, in the long run, disastrous.

*

At least one churchman was not satisfied with the decision of Alexander IV, and tried to do something about it. This was bishop Florent, the one who had provided the Anagni commission with long excerpts from Joachim's works. The bishop of St-Jean d'Acre was made archbishop of Arles, in Provence, by pope Urban IV (1261-1264) in 1262, possibly in acknowledgement of his services in the Anagni Commission. Shortly after moving to his new see in the Fall of 1263 the archbishop called and presided a provincial synod. Although the exact date is uncertain, it is usually designated as the synod of 1263. The first item on the agenda aimed at doing what the General Councils of the century (Lateran IV in 1215, and Lyon I in 1245) and the bishops of Rome had failed to do. Florent stood by the Protocol of Anagni in its integrity. He was determined to condemn Joachim's doctrine, *Joachitica doctrina*, especially as it was flourishing among *Joachitici*, the followers of the visionary abbot. While other synodal decisions dealt with local concerns in the archdiocese of Arles, the condemnation of Joachimism was the real purpose of the gathering.

The decrees of the synod are introduced by a preface in which the Joachimites are said to place Joachim's "stinking doctrine in the nefarious context of his concordances and his malicious veneration of the Holy Spirit[27]." This doctrine is denounced as an attempt, through "a fictitious intermingling of some trilogies, to demonstrate that the times of the Holy Spirit will soon be revealed, along with a better Law[28]." Joachim also maintained that there are "three *status* or orders of men...", and an "Eternal Gospel or Gospel of the Holy Spirit," which he "fantastically" claimed to find symbolized by the two wheels in Isaiah's prophetic vision of the Seraphim (Is. 6:2). In keeping with this description of Joachim's false doctrines, canon I of the synod decreed:

> We therefore,... in sofar as we must and can..., by the authority of our sacred provincial council, reproving the aforesaid teachings as they have come to our hands, lest our subjects use such notions and receive more, do outlaw them permanently with anathema[29].

The Holy See, meanwhile, persevered in its astonishing silence about Joachim. It never endorsed the anathema of the Arlesian synod. In spite of recurring defiance by diverse groups of Spiritual Franciscans, the popes continued implicitly to tolerate Joachim's aberrant views on the Church and, worse, on the divine Trinity. They showed more concern with Guillaume de St-Amour's denunciation of the friars as the perils of the last days and with its immediate occasion, Gherardo da Borgo San Donnino's use of Joachim's prophecies, than with the heresies at the heart of Joachim's theology, that were the basis of Gherardo's aberrant views. Constitution 2 of Lateran Council IV had been a mild slap on the hand, since it left untouched Joachim's view of the Three Persons and his detailed sketch of the trinitarian structure of history. It was precisely this theory that obtained a willing audience among the Friars Minor, under the protection, if not the encouragement, of Giovanni da Parma.

*

That Joachim stirred the imagination of contemporary poets is hardly surprising. What seems odd is that the proper judgment was expressed by a rather secular author, Robert de Meung (c.1240-c.1305), in the second part of the *Roman de la Rose*, while Dante Alighieri (1265-1321), renowned for his religious poetry, completely distorted the situation. As he told the story of the selling of Gherardo's book in Paris, Robert de Meung made it clear that the book ought to be burned in front of Notre-Dame, the very place where it had been peddled by Gherardo and his friends:

> ...To obtain a copy
> Of a book from the great devil
> Called the everlasting gospel
> Ministered by the Holy Spirit...
> (*...Pour bailler comme exemplaire*

Un livre de par le grand diable
Dit l'évangile perdurable
Dont le Saint-Esprit fut ministre[30]...

There are also heavy traces of the memory of Joachim in the works of Rutebeuf (1245-c.1285), another *trouvère* who was familiar with the Parisian scene. Rutebeuf, enamored of the old ways of the Church, agreed with Guillaume de Saint-Amour, and regarded the powers given to the friars as an intolerable novelty. He was in fact much more vehement against the Dominicans (*la gent Dominique*) than against the Franciscans. He held the Friars preachers responsible for "invading" the university of Paris, defended the vanishing monopolies of the secular clergy, and openly blamed king Louis IX for the exile of Guillaume de Saint-Amour in 1257, and for his support of the Mendicants. Without naming Joachim he described the friars in terms that fit the abbot more directly. In a poem composed in the second half of 1259, Rutebeuf also alluded to "the fifth evangelist," to "a new epistle[31]," a probable allusion to a letter that was signed by the two Ministers general in 1255. He accused Dominicans and Franciscans of behaving toward God like an Inquisitor in a torture chamber: "You are ministers, not masters, / you cut God's right ear[32]..." The clergy who failed to protest were seriously guilty: "You abandon the Holy Scripture[33]..." First among them was the pope, Alexander IV, who was also severely castigated by the poet.

At the same time, Rutebeuf was enthusiastic for the crusades and the new Latin dominions in the East. He praised Louis IX for embarking for the Holy Land. Like popes Urban IV (1261-1264) and Clement IV (1265-1268), who regarded the campaigns of Louis IX's brother, Charles d'Anjou, against Manfred as a holy war, Rutebeuf favored a crusade in Sicily. True knights risk their life for the Holy Sepulcher and the Church, while ambitious, self-seeking, and hypocritical preachers claim poverty in order to live off the substance of others. In a poem that bemoaned the reconquest of Constantinople by the Greek emperor Michael Paleologos on July 25, 1261, Rutebeuf called the Friars "inventors of a new belief, a new God and a new gospel[34]," terms that are clearly reminiscent of Gherardo da Borgo San Donnino and, beyond him, of Joachim and his predictions.

In Italy, meanwhile, Dante Alighieri, who was not above using theology for political purposes[35], aligned himself for once with the papal protectors of Joachim. He even depicted Thomas and Bonaventure as admirers of the Calabrian. In *Paradiso*, canto IX, he made the ghost of Thomas Aquinas speak in quasi-Joachimite language. God sent "two captains" to the Church his Spouse, with the mission to act as her guides. It is easy to recognize Francis and Dominic in these lines:

L'un fu tutto serafico in ardore;
l'altro per sapïenza in terra fue
di cherubica luce uno splendore
(The one was all seraphic heart a-glow,
the other by the wisdom he attained
a splendor of cherubic light below[36]).

At this point Dante added lengthy praises of Francis and Lady Poverty. At the end of Canto XII he extolled Dominic and other theologians who dwell in the same heavenly circle: Hugh of St. Victor, Peter Comestor, Peter of Spain (pope John XXI), the prophet Nathan (2 Kings 7), John Chrysostom, Anselm, Donato, a fourth-century grammarian whose works were studied through the Middle Ages[37], Rabanus (776-856), archbishop of Mainz, often celebrated as *praeceptor Germaniae*, "the preceptor of Germany." Finally there is, as the ghostly Bonaventure is made to say,

... lucemi da lato
il calavrese abate Giovacchino,
de spirito profetico dotato
(... shining at my side,
the Calabrian abbot Joachim,
gifted with the prophetic spirit[38]).

There is a wide discrepancy between this pseudo-Bonaventurian praise of Joachim and what the living Bonaventure actually wrote. As we shall see, the Seraphic Doctor considered Joachim a false prophet. Reputations, however, are slow to evolve when they confirm a deep desire that is widespread in the Christian people. The irrational expectation that eschatological promises, anticipations, or dreams will soon become historical happenings is fed by a fundamental nisus toward a better life on this earth. It has remained one of Christianity's recurrent problems. Controlling the theological answer to this desire remains a permanent tasks of the Church. The attempt to control lingering Joachimite expectations among the Christian people, however, has been far from entirely successful.

*

Was it by mere happenstance that the false prophecies of Joachim regarding the Eternal Gospel were echoed by sectarian movements through the rest of the Middle Ages and far into modern times? When Boniface VIII decreed special indulgences for the pilgrims who would travel to Rome in the year 1300, for the opening of the fourteenth century (bull *Antiquorum habet fida relatio*), he was making a belated effort to channel the energies unleashed by Joachim and Gherardo da Borgo San Donnino. This was the first Christian reenactment of the biblical jubilees. Though this term was not in the bull, it was widely used by chroniclers and commentators who described the event.

As it echoed the Jubilees of the Old Testament, the pilgrimage to Rome in 1300 signified both the reconciliation of sinners and enemies, and the replacement of Jerusalem by Rome. It projected a new image of the End Times, which so many people, trusting Joachim's prophecies, still expected for the near future. The hopes in an Eternal Gospel soon to come that Joachim had kindled were wisely channeled by Boniface toward a deeper appropriation of the Gospel of Christ, the only Eternal Gospel, in its reconciling and forgiving power. The pope himself was so aware of this significance that, unwilling to be reconciled with those he regarded as his worst enemies, he uncharitably issued another bull, *Nuper per alias*, to specify that the indulgences of 1300 were applicable neither to Frederick II of Aragon (d.1337), king of Sicily since 1296, nor to members of the wealthy and influential Colonna family, at the time his most determined political adversaries in Rome[39]! That Boniface was setting a bad example of spiritual discrimination was an unfortunate incident, which did not, however, ruin the general intent and meaning of the Jubilee of 1300.

Notes

1 Wessley, *Joachim...*, p. 71, note 3.

2 H. Denifle and F. Ehrle, *"Protocoll der Commission zu Anagni"* (*Archiv für Literatur und Reformationsgeschichte des Mittelalters*, vol. I, Berlin, 1885, reprinted, Graz, 1955, p.99-142: the Protocol is introduced by a long study, "*Das Evangelium aeternum und die Commission zu Anagni*", p.49-98), text, p.102; Panidensis is certainly Panion, also called Panis, or Phanorion, in the ecclesiastical province of Heraclea (Michael Lequien, *Oriens Christianus*, vol. III, reprint, Graz: Akademische Verlaganstalt, 1958, p.966), though Giorgio Fedalto locates it in the province of Europe, diocese of Thrace (*Le Chiese d'Oriente*, vol. 2, Milan: Jaca books, 1993, p.75); Bonevaletus is the Latinized form of a name that has not been identified further; given the task of the Commission and the presence in Constantinople, from 1204 to 1261, of an illegitimate Latin Emperor, it seems probable that this bishop was not Greek.

3 Denifle-Ehrle, "*Protocoll...*," p.99.

4 *...eo tempore quo Spiritus Sanctus proprietate misterii operatur* (p.100).

5 P.101.

6 P.102.

7 The foundation is examined p.102-105; citation, p.102-103.

8 P.105.

9 P.105-115.

10 P.115-120.

11 P.115.

12 P.120-126.

13 P.120.

14 P.126-136.

15 P.126.

16 P.126-130.

17 P.130-133: *...dominum Jesum Christum, qui apparuit in principio secundi status cum apostolis suis, esse figuram et similitudinem cujusdam venturi cum suis in principio tertii status* (p.130).

18 P.133-136.

19 P.136-142.

20 P.137.

21 P.140.

22 P.142.

23 P. 141.

24 *Eum fuisse virum catholicum reputamus, et regularem observantiam quam instituit salutarem* (*Regesta Honorii Papae*, vol. I, n. 2881, p. 26).

25 *Mandat ut in defensionem monachorum de ordine Floris publicent abbatum Joachim non fuisse haereticum...; sed, quum omnia scripta sua mandaverit Pontifici assignari, Apostolico judicio approbanda seu etiam corrigenda, et*

confessus sit se illam fidem tenere quam Romana tenet Ecclesia (*Regesta Honorii...*, vol. II, n. 2881, p. 476-477).

26 *Quia vero prae angustia temporum non potui hucusque opuscula ipsa, praeter Concordiam, Apostolico culmine praesentare...* (Bollandists, *Acta sanctorum*, May, vol. VII, p. 102).

27 Text in Mansi, *Conciliorum... amplissima collectio*, vol.XXIII, col.1001-1002; citation, col. 1002; most of the text is reproduced in de Lubac, *La Postérité...*, vol. 1, appendix B, p.400-405.

28 Mansi, col.1003.

29 Mansi, col.1004; Henri de Lubac insists that Joachim is not named in the acts of Arles (*La Postérité...*, vol. 1, p. 402); the omission of his name, however, is largely insignificant, since Joachim's works are clearly indicated as the source of the *Joachiticis*' errors.

30 Jean de Meung, *Le Roman de la Rose, dans la version attribuée à Clément Marot*, vol.2, Milan: Istituto Editoriale Cisalpino, 1957, p.223; the story goes from verse 12162 to 12302.

31 "*Le Dit de Sainte Eglise*" (Edmond Farral and Julia Bastin, eds., *Oeuvres complètes de Rutebeuf*, 2 vol., Paris: Editions Picard, 1959), vol. I, p.277-285: The text is in medieval French: ...*Quant le cinqueime evengelitre/ Vost on fere mestre et menistre/ De parler du roi celestre.../ Cil qui font la novelle espitre...* (p.280).

32 *Vous estes mitres non pas mestre:/ Vous copez Dieu l'oroille destre...*

33 *Il est bien raison et droiture/ Vous laissiez la sainte Ecriture/ Dont sainte Eglise est deconfite*! (p.282).

34 "*Complainte de Constantinople*" (*Oeuvres complètes...*, vol. I, p.426): *Et fera nueve remanance/ à cela qui font nueve creance,/ Novel Dieu et nueve Evangile...*; the Latin emperor Baldwin II took refuge in France; he was of course an intruder.

35 See Ernest Fortin, *Dissidence et philosophie au moyen âge. Dante et ses antécédents*, Montreal: Bellarmin, 1981; *Dantes Göttliche Komödie als Utopie*, Munich: Piper, 1989; "Dante and the Politics of Christendom," in J. Brian Benestad, ed., *The Birth of Philosophical Christianity. Studies in Early Christian and Medieval Thought. Ernest Fortin's Collected Essays*, vol. I (New York: Rowman and Littlefield, 1996), p. 251-305.

36 Alberto Chiari, ed., *La Divina Commedia,* Milan: Bietti, 1977, p. 484; translation by Laurence Bynion, in Paolo Milano, ed., *Portable Dante*, New York: Viking Press, 1976, Canto XI, 37-39 (text in Chiari, *La Divina...*, p. 422).

37 This would seem odd if one did not know that the name of Dante's wife was Gemma Donati!

38 Canto XI, v.139-141 (Chiari, *La Divina...*, p.495; Milano, *Portable Dante*, p. 431).

39 E. M. Jung-Inglessis, *Romfahrt durch zwei Jahrtausende*, Rome: Athesiadruck, 1976, p. 35-45.

Chapter 5
The Judgment of Thomas Aquinas

If Gherardo's lucubrations seriously threatened the Franciscan self-understanding, they were also a danger for all the communities that had been formed in the first decades of the thirteenth century, in keeping with the regulations of Lateran Council IV. The conciliar Constitution 13 had expressed the fear that the creation of new Orders could cause confusion. It had therefore decided that new communities must adopt one of the existing rules and structures rather than invent new ones. In the West this meant, in practice, the older rules of St. Augustine and St. Benedict. In practice the more recent rule of St. Francis was tolerated, Francis's original "Form of Life" being composed in 1212/1213, though the official rules came later: The so-called "primitive" rule of 1221, and the "second" of 1223, that was canonically approved by pope Honorius III, were adaptations of it. The decision of the council did not in fact preempt all confusion. The Friars were also exposed to another kind of danger when their involvement in the university of Paris triggered Guillaume de St-Amour's onslaught against them. This was especially felt among the Friars preachers of St. Dominic.

The dates are intriguing. Humbert de Romans[1] (c.1200-1277) was elected Master general on 13 May 1254, after an interregnum of one year and a half (his predecessor John Teutonicus had died on 4 November 1252). This was just about the time when the *Liber introductorius* became known. The new Master general had presumably little leisure to make a sober assessment of Gherardo's contentions. He was concerned at the considerable tension that was festering between Dominicans and Franciscans. They had been created at about the same time, with a common evangelical purpose, though with different accents, that were on doctrinal preaching by the former, on the example of evangelical poverty by the latter. They found themselves to be rivals in many places, trying to attract the same people. They both had received the privilege of lecturing at the university of Paris, but the Preachers held two chairs of theology, the Friars minor only one.

*

Humbert de Romans was, if anything, clear-sighted. He saw the rivalry of the new Orders as a weakness when they faced the hostility of the secular clergy, and especially of those who, with Guillaume de St. Amour, judged their teaching privileges exorbitant and derogatory for the traditional priesthood of the secular clergy. Shortly after his election he ordered the Dominicans to moderate their attitudes in regard to the seculars, and even to give up claiming some of their rights. He also did his utmost to ensure fraternity between Dominicans and Franciscans, and this, partly in response to an invitation from Innocent IV. This pope was adamant in affirming the superiority of the spiritual over the temporal power, claiming the right to depose kings and relentlessly opposing Emperor Frederick II. He was also a particularly determined hunter of heretics. In the bull *Ad extirpendam* (15 May 1252) he authorized the use of torture by the Inquisition, with the qualification that it should not cause dismemberment or death. In *Cum adversus* (22 February 1254) he came out in favor of putting hardened heretics to death, using the sword «against the enemies of the faith and for the extermination of heretical depravity, that the viper-like sons of perfidy who insult God and the Church, evil-doers, be not allowed to live.» He was therefore eager that the two Orders he chiefly relied on for the Inquisition would not indirectly help the enemies of the faith by wasting their energies in incongruous rivalries. In several documents he advised them not to steal each other's candidates, and in a joint letter to Dominicans and Franciscans he urged them to live and act as brothers[2]. He nevertheless was sufficiently impressed by Guillaume de Saint-Amour's complaints and arguments that, in *Etsi animarum* (21 November 1254), a few weeks before he died, he restricted somewhat the privileges previously granted to the Friars. [2]

Humbert and Giovanni da Perma did their best to promote fraternity. In Milan in February 1255, less than a year after the appearance of the *Liber introductorius*, the two ministers general issued a joint letter, *Salvator mundi*, in which they reviewed the task of their Orders at the service of the Church. In this they indeed affirmed the providential role of their communities. They did so, however, in extravagant language that bordered on the apocalyptic. Although no mention was made of either Joachim or Gherardo, this language could be understood as endorsing the belief that their mission had eschatological significance. It was not enough for them to affirm the fraternity of the two Orders of Dominic and Francis. They did not hesitate to claim, "for the glory of God," to be part of a long biblical tradition of twin brotherhood. They were "the two great luminaries..., the two trumpets of the true Moses, Christ our God..., the two Cherubim, full of knowledge, contemplating each other..." They were also "the two breasts of the bride, at which those who are children in Christ suck the milk by which they are fed and they receive increases in salvation." They were "the two sons of beauty of the olive, who assist the Lord of the universal earth," and also "the two witnesses of Christ...," and "those two brilliant stars which, according to the Sybilline prophecy, bear the faces of four animals, shouting in these last days in the name of the Lamb, in the direction of humility and voluntary poverty[3].»

If not the intent, at least the language that Humbert de Romans favored, hinted at the apocalyptic significance of the Friars. When the troubles between the secular Masters and the Friars developed at the University of Paris, a letter he addressed to the Friars preachers in Orléans sounded just as pompous, if not arrogant, in its claims for the Friars preachers. The adversary who is hindering their work in Paris is no less than «Satan,... Leviathan, the tortuous snake,... Belial, the enemy of justice, fighter against innocence,... a ferocious and furious wildboar... When meeting face to face on the streets we are insulted with Christ, we suffer blows, we are attacked, we are ambushed, fought against, cursed...» He compared them further with Abel opposed by Caïn, with Joseph, with «the chosen people of God» persecuted by Aman, with David, with Peter, Paul, John and the deacon Stephen[4]... It is hardly surprising that such extravagant comparisons were offensive to many, and that in consequence the Friars in some quarters acquired a reputation of intolerable arrogance. In his massive chronicle of England, the Benedictine Matthew Paris, of the abbey of St. Alban, accused them generally of living in luxury. He accused the Dominicans of «usurping the task of ordinaries and showing contempt for them as leading the people of God and regulating the cinctures of the Church while they are deficient in knowledge and strength.» He blamed two Franciscans, for «extorting money for the work of Lord Pope» in the year 1247. Given the general anxiety that seems to have been pervasive in Western Europe in the thirteenth century, such a reputation, true or false, could easily fit in an expectation of the coming end of the world.

Precisely, the claim to a new and special vocation that was neither secular nor monastic played into the hands of Guillaume de St-Amour, when he searched for arguments against the presence of the Friars at the university of Paris. There was in fact a bitter polemic against the followers of St. Dominic. It even left heavy traces in the vernacular literature of the thirteenth century in France. A wild rumor that some Dominicans had composed the *Liber introductorius ad evangelium aeternum* was even reported by Matthew Paris, who apparently believed it to be true. The poet Ruteboeuf, whom we have already met, was mostly hostile to the Dominicans. The resignation of Humbert de Romans in 1263 was not unrelated to the continuing turmoil around possible connections between the Friars and the wild theology of Gherardo. The Preachers, however, were saved from a widespread Joachimite interpretation of their calling by Thomas Aquinas's immediate and unambiguous opposition to Joachim's theology.

The strictures of Guillaume de St-Amour against the practice of evangelical poverty by the Friars were answered by Aquinas, Bonaventure, and others, and it is possible that many among the Friars deemed Guillaume more dangerous to them than Joachim and Gherardo. While their abundant refutation of Guillaume's contentions fall outside the time frame of our immediate topic, the judgment of the two great scholastics on Joachim's eschatology is essential both to an assessment of the doctrines of the Calabrian, and to an evaluation of the extent to which pope Alexander IV departed from the prevailing theological opinion when he failed to draw attention to the underlying heterodoxy of Joachim's doctrines. Thomas and Bonaventure were in total agreement in their conclusions, though their methods of approach differed.

The theologians, however, had to proceed with caution. In May, July, and August of 1254, after the initial complaints of Guillaume de St. Amour against the Friars and the claims of Gherardo about the Eternal Gospel, pope Innocent IV issued a series of bulls that restricted the privileges granted the Friars by Honorius III. Innocent was not opposed to the Friars as such. While he initiated their missions to Prussia and Pomerania, however, he also wanted, as a devoted canonist, to protect the traditional status of the diocesan clergy. His efforts in this sense culminated in a bull, *Etsi animarum*, of 21 November 1254, which, had it been systematically applied, would have placed most of the Friars' activities under the supervision of the secular clergy. This appeared at first as an unmitigated success for the adversaries of the Friars. Pope Innocent, however, died three weeks later, on 7 December. His successor Alexander IV adopted a different policy. On 22 December 1254, that is, as soon as he was elected, Alexander issued a bull, *Nec insolitum*, in which he suspended the application of Innocent's decrees, and even declared that Innocent had acted hastily, an unusual criticism of a pope by his immediate successor! On 14 April 1255, after the joint letter from the two Masters general, pope Alexander issued another bull, *Quasi lignum vitae*, by which he definitely restored all the privileges that had been extended to the Friars by Honorius III.

*

Aquinas was quite hostile to Joachim from the start of his career. Since the reputation of the Calabrian abbot had been deflated by Lateran Council IV, there was little urgency to refute his ideas before Gherardo da Borgo San Donnino issued his manifesto, and a type of Joachimism exploded in the Franciscan communities. In 1252, nevertheless, in the conclusion of his *Principium*[5], an address on the structures of the Scriptures that he gave when he was made a bachelor in the Bible at the university of Paris, the young Thomas divided the time of the Church in three moments. *Initium*, the beginning, is recorded in the Acts of the Apostles. *Progressus*, the development, is described in the canonical epistles, and it follows the "apostolic instruction" that they contain. *Terminus*, the end, is evoked in the Apocalypse, which brings "the content of all the Sacred Scripture" to conclusion. This threefold division evidently eliminated Joachim's focus on the Apocalypse as the prophetic key to the Church' s future.

In spite of the various millennarist movements that have sprung up from time to time, the last book of the Bible does not look directly forward to the future. It looks backward to the past and to previous Scriptures, on which its expectation of the future and the eschaton is based.

Having established the basic scriptural principle of his understanding of the Church, Aquinas hardly referred to Joachim in his *Commentary on the Sentences of Peter Lombard.* In book III he faced a question that had some prominence in Joachim's theories: Did Jesus love the apostle John more than he loved Peter? Thomas's yes-and-no answer is a model of conciliation: "Peter was more loved by Christ as to interior affection ... and John was better loved as to signs of public familiarity[6]." Since the fourth book of the Commentary was composed in 1256, some two years after Gherardo's *Liber introductorius ad evangelium aeternum*, one might expect Thomas to show hostility to those of Joachim's ideas that were at the origin of Gherardo's speculations. In fact, he openly blamed Joachim for the excessive reaction of Guillaume de St-Amour, who judged the prophetic announcement of a new and eternal Gospel to be the first sign that Antichrist has arrived and is at work: "This Gospel of which they speak is a certain introduction included in a book of Joachim that has been rejected by the Church. Or it is Joachim's own doctrine, by which, they say, the Gospel of Christ has been changed[7]".

Thomas also had the occasion to speak of Joachim when, in the *Commentary on the Sentences*, he explained the «state of the new Law[8]." Because, he argued, the key to the Scriptures is given between the old Law and the heavenly homeland, those things that pertain to the new Law are, on one side, the truth of the signs given in the old Law, on the other side, images (*figurae*) of the manifest and full knowledge of the ultimate truth in the homeland. This was the common doctrine. It was not that of Joachim, for whom the full knowledge of the truth will be given in the soon-to-come Eternal Gospel of the Holy Spirit. Thomas's use of the word *figura*, that occurs frequently under Joachim's pen, openly suggests that Thomas had him in mind as one who misrepresented the status of the new Law. Although he refrained at this point from naming the abbot or directly contradicting his recent followers, Thomas was striking at the heart of the Joachimite problematic.

Thomas in fact contradicted Joachim by name in other opuscula. The refutation of Joachim was at the center of Thomas's commentary on Lateran IV: *In decretalem secundam expositio.* He actually read more, in the decree against Joachim, than the council itself had specified. Not only did he regard the abbot as a stupid man, who quoted authorities that he did not understand. Not only was Joachim wrong in his critique of Peter Lombard, but this critique itself shows that Joachim's doctrine of the Trinity was patently erroneous. Instead of confessing «the unity of essence of the Three Persons» as «true, real, and simple,» Joachim held the Three Persons to be one «as though by similarity and collectively, that is, as though gathered from many, as many men are said to be one people, and many believers one church[9]." This amounted, in Thomas's opinion, to the heresy of Arianism. At least it logically followed from Arius's contention that the divine Logos is no more than a transcendent creature, who may be called divine by similarity with God. Thomas did not mention, and he possibly did not know, that even with his notable errors Joachim could not be called, like Arius, a hardened heretic, since he had professed to submit his writings to the judgment of the Apostolic See.

In his defense of the Friars against Guillaume de St-Amour (*Contra impugnantes Dei cultum et religionem*), composed after the publication of Guillaume's vitriolic attack of 1255, Thomas realized that it was not sufficient to refute Guillaume 's accusations and argue that the two orders of Dominic and Francis were not "the perils of the last days." The hostility of Guillaume to the Friars he regarded as intruders in the University was fed by the wild claims of the *Liber introductorius* and by Gherardo's view of Francis as the herald of the Eternal Gospel. In order to be effective, the refutation of Guillaume's judgment had to strike at the root of criticism of the Friars, that is, at Gherardo's application of Joachim's categories to Francis of Assisi. Guillaume was in fact using Joachim's idea that the last days were imminent. He of course did not expect the major apocalyptic event that Joachim had projected for the year 1260 or thereabouts. Rather, he considered that the time of Antichrist had arrived, and that the sign of its presence was Joachim's expectation of the "gospel that they call eternal.» After devoting twenty-three chapters to a refutation of Guillaume's pointed criticisms of the friars, Thomas's *Contra impugnantes* therefore focused two chapters on the coming of the Antichrist. Joachim is named. All predictions of the time of the Antichrist are declared to be contrary to the New Testament (Acts 1, 7). Thomas clearly identified this expectation with the doctrine of Joachim.

It was in the *Summa theologica*, begun in 1266, therefore after the fatidic date of 1260 had come and gone without fulfilling the Joachimite prophecies, that Thomas' s opposition to Joachim was the most fundamental. Indeed the method of *concordia* provided a good reason to specify, at the start of the *Summa theologiae*, that only from the literal sense of Scripture can one draw valid theological arguments. Although Joachim is not named in this methodological *questio*, much of the discussion aims at those who abuse the spiritual senses of Scripture. Joachim's elaborate analysis of senses and types was an extremely artificial development of the allegorical exegesis that had been practiced in monastic theology since the *Moralia in Job* of Gregory the Great (c.540-604). That Joachim was not generally followed was due to the inherent safeguards of the hermeneutic tradition, to which the great scholastics, and notably Thomas, were more sensitive than he was, these safeguards making sure that the theological virtues, faith, hope, and love, acted as the standards of the spiritual senses. After declaring that philosophical disciplines do not constitute the whole of human knowledge (a. l), showing in what sense Holy Scripture is a type of *scientia* (a. 2) and explaining what kind it is (a. 3-7), Thomas discusses the arguments that may be used in theology (a. 8-10). All this section of the *Summa* reads like a scarcely-disguised anti-Joachimite pamphlet.

In article 8, the angelic doctor explains that «this doctrine» (the *scientia* of divine revelation in Scripture) does not prove the truth of its principles, but receives the truth from the articles of faith, which function as its "first principles." In other words, theologians look to the traditional creeds for testing their views. It is indeed proper for Scripture to use metaphors (a. 9) and for commentators to investigate the spiritual senses that may hide under the literal (a. 10). At this point, where Joachim and his followers would have esteemed their researches justified, Aquinas places his statement that the validity of a theological argument rests entirely on the literal sense of Scripture[10] . All speculations about a *concordia* of the two Testaments that would reveal the key to the apocalyptic future are therefore vain exercises, and Joachim's *concordia* proves nothing at all. Thomas is of course familiar with the old practice of monastic theology, and he admits the traditional senses of Scripture. History states facts; etiology assigns causes; analogy compares differing passages and shows their harmony; allegory looks for lessons to be drawn in the areas of faith (typology), of love (tropology), and of hope (anagogy). This multiplicity of senses does not destroy the value and the theological meaning of the literal sense. That the term used by Thomas for typology is, again, *figura,* is hardly accidental. It was one of Joachim' s favorite terms, by which the abbot designated the anticipation of the New Testament in the Old, the figuration of the eschaton in the New Testament, and his own imaginative drawings of his intellectual conceptions. Thomas redirects *figura* in a more traditional direction.

Elsewhere in the *Summa,* as he refutes the notion that in God the "essence generates the essence[11]," Thomas explicitly attributes this false conception to Joachim and he explicitly contradicts one of the implications of Joachim's Trinitarian views. In the *Disputed Questions de Potentia* he denies both that "one should know in advance precisely the time of the second advent[12]," and that "another state that leads to perfection will succeed the Law of the Gospel, as it itself succeeded the old Law, and the old Law succeeded the law of nature[13]." Thus the possibility of a third age of the Church is denied, and this is directly opposed to Joachim's eschatology.

Thomas Aquinas undoubtedly ruined any influence that the apocalyptic theories of the abbot of Fiore could have had on scholastic theology. After the flare up at the university of Paris in the mid-thirteenth century Christian scholarship was happily free from speculation on a transformist ecclesiology tied to an imminent eschatology. As he thus enlarged the horizon of the debate, Thomas did not wish to honor Joachim's doctrines by giving them undue importance. Neither were the last days around the corner, nor was Joachim so impressive a figure as to be himself a herald of Antichrist. Thomas rejected the idea that the doctrine of Joachim or of his introductor, Gherardo, is the doctrine that Antichrist will preach, although it contains other points that must be rejected. If one understands Antichrist to be in favor of every false doctrine, a false doctrine as such is not an unmistakable sign of the his imminent reign. There has in fact been no time since the primitive church in which heretical doctrines have not been put forward.

Thomas attacked Joachim, explicitly or implicitly, in other passages of his works. As he reflected on Hebr. 9, 5 in his Commentary on the Epistle to the Hebrews, he unequivocally affirmed that «the final age is the present time, after which there will not be another time of salvation,» a clearly anti-Joachimite statement. Similar texts are found in Thomas's other biblical commentaries. Around 1259, just before the Joachimite expectation for 1260 could be fulfilled, more objections to Joachim were formulated in Quodlibetal question 7. As was said by St. Jerome, "the state of the Church is between the state of the Synagogue and that of the Church triumphant[14]." Since the meaning of the Scriptures is commensurate with the state of the Church when they were composed, one must also affirm:

> The Old Testament was the figure of the New; the Old and the New together are the figure of the heavenly realities. A spiritual sense oriented toward proper faith may be founded in that mode of figuration by which the Old Testament signifies the New; and this is the allegorical or typical sense, according to which the events of the Old Testament are applied to Christ and the Church; or it can be founded in that mode of figuration by which the New and the Old together signify the Church triumphant; and this is the anagogical sense[15].

In other words, Joachim's reading of the Apocalypse was, in spite of his contention regarding his quasi-miraculous discovery of *spiritualis intellectus*, excessively literal. And if indeed theological arguments must be supported by the literal sense of the Bible, literality in interpreting the spiritual sense of Scripture is both a contradiction and the mark of a small mind. Joachim in any case did not understand the authorities he argued from[16].

The Joachimite exegesis gave the impression of great subtlety. Joachim had invested an extraordinary amount of persistence into his search for point by point correspondences between the events of the Old Testament and those of the New. This had led him to posit twelve spiritual senses of the text and a remarkable *concordia* between the Old and the New taken as interlocking historical periods. His designation of the time of king Josiah as an anticipated beginning of the New Testament, however, showed a major difference between his methodology and the standard tradition of Christian hermeneutics. And what Joachim identified as the spiritual sense or senses of the letter was far from the straightforward simplicity of the scholastic reading. The twelve spiritual senses that were explained at length in the *Concordia* were obtained by adding seven kinds (*species*) of senses to five interpretations that Joachim professed to find in the hermeneutic tradition. These five were listed as historical, moral, tropological, contemplative, and anagogical. They were obtained by subdividing two of the senses that were identified in the traditional quatrain:

> The letter teaches facts, allegory what to believe,
> morality what to do, anagogy what to aim at.
> (*Littera gesta docet, quid credas allegoria,*
> *Moralis quid agas, quo tendas anagogia*[17]).

Joachim unfolded the letter into two, for one should distinguish between the very matter of penmanship (the ink, with its color and shape) and the literal or historical sense that is conveyed by the script. He further divided the moral sense into two, moral strictly taken (relating to ethical choices) and tropological (which metaphorically designates another reality than what the letter conveys). His tropology was in fact very close to what most scholastics called allegorical. Finally, Joachim divided the traditional anagogy in two by distinguishing the contemplative sense from the anagogical. He grounded this distinction in the nature of the *transitus*, the passage, through which the faithful go from earthly to heavenly concerns. Understanding is contemplative when, "the flesh being abandoned, it passes in spirit" to a point where what is perceived is quite other than what is read. Then Hagar, Abraham's slave in Genesis 16, becomes the active life, and Sara, the free woman, the contemplative life. Understanding is anagogical when it is the reader, rather than the meaning, who undergoes an inner transformation and learns "to despise earthly things and to love heavenly things." In addition to these six senses Joachim discovered a typological or comparative sense (*sensus typicus*), that he subdivided into seven modes, which themselves were patterned on the interrelationships of the Three Persons. Reading the biblical text in light of the Three divine Persons, Father, Son, and Holy Spirit, gave him three "types," modes, or senses. Three more were obtained by comparing the text with the relations between the Father and the Son, the Father and the Spirit, the Son and the Spirit. A seventh and final type was reached by applying the text to the Trinity as a whole.

*

That there was a fallacy in the system was not immediately apparent. And this may explain why Joachim got so many followers. The fallacy derived from Joachim's overlooking of a fundamental principle. The traditional Trinitarian doctrine does not allow for a contemplation of the Trinity that would be other than the contemplation of the Father/Logos/Spirit relationships. The Trinity is neither other than the Three Persons, nor other than the one divine Being. In the theology that Augustine had passed on to the Middle Ages, the Persons are their relationships, a point that was developed more technically by Thomas Aquinas. The Joachimite fallacy implicitly posited an epistemic distinction between the Three Persons and the Trinity. This error was not radically different from what Joachim accused Peter Lombard of doing: He saw the Trinity as a quaternity. Because the Lateran Council, however, as it rebutted this critique of the Lombard in its Second Decree, drew conclusions from what Joachim had written without quoting his own words, it remained at the level of interpretation. And so it could not fully unveil the basic fallacy of Joachimism. In reality, Joachim's determination of multiple biblical senses besides those that had become traditional warped the contemplation of the divine Three, as though the Persons could be paired two by two at the whim of the contemplative, and thus each escape in some way from the normative Trinity. Each Person, on the contrary, immediately implies the entire Trinitarian horizon.

Notes

1 Edward Tracy Brett, *Humbert de Romans. His Life and Views of thirteenth-century Society,* Toronto: Pontifical Institute of Medieval Studies, 1984, p. 9-24.

2 Letter of Innocent IV... Luke Wadding, *Annales Minorum*, vol. 5, Quaracchi, 1931, p. 383-384.

3 Text in Wadding, *Annales...*, vol. 3, p. 429; also in *Monumenta Ordinis Praedicatorum Historica,* vol. 16 (1935), p. 369.

4 Henry Richards Luard, ed., *Matthaei Parisiensis Chronica majora*, 7 vol., London: Longman, 1872-1883, vol. 4, see p. 279, 511, 599.

5 Petrus Mandonnet, ed., *Sancti Thomae Aquinatis Opuscula Omnia*, vol. 4, 1927, p.490.

6 *...quantum ad signa exterioris familiaritatis* (*Commentary on the Sentences* III, d. 3l, q. 2, a. 3, sol. 3). Most of Thomas's references to Joachim are indicated in Henri de Lubac, *Postérité...*, vol. l, p. 144-155.

7 *... cum quidam jam Christi evangelium mutare conentur in quoddam aliud evangelium quod dicunt aeternum, manifeste dicunt instare tempora Antichristi. Hoc autem evangelium de quo loquuntur est quoddam introductorium in libro Joachim compositum. Vel etiam ipsa doctrina Joachim, per quam, ut dicunt, Evangelium Christi mutatur.* (*Contra impugnantes Dei cultum et religionem,* ch. 24, in Mandonnet, *Opuscula...*, vol. 4, p. 185).

8 *Status novae legis medius est inter statum veteris legis et statum coelestis patriae; et ideo etiam quae sunt novae legis, et sunt veritas respectu signorum veteris legis, et sunt figurae respectu manifestae et planae cognitionis veritatis quae erit in patria; et ideo adhuc oportet in nova lege quod maneant aliquae figurae...* (CS IV, d. l, q. l, a. 2, sol. 5).

9 *Non enim ponebat unitatem essentiae trium personarum esse veram, realem et simplicem, sed quasi similitudinariam et collectivam, id est, quasi e pluribus congregatam, sicut multi homines dicuntur unus populus et multi fideles dicuntur una ecclesia* (*In decretalem secundam expositio*, in Mandonnet, *Opuscula...*, vol. 4, p. 343-344).

10 S. T., I, q.1, a.1, ad l

11 S. T., I, q. 39, a.5.

12 *Q. D. de Potentia*, q. 5, a. 6, ad 7 (Mandonnet, *Quaestiones disputatae*, vol. 2, 1925, p. 193).

13 *De Potentia*, q. 5, a. 6, ad 9 (p. 193-194).

14 *Status ecclesiae medius est inter statum synagogae et statum ecclesiae triumphantis* (quoted by Thomas in *Quodlibetal Question* 7, a. 15 : Mandonnet, *Quaestiones quodlibetales*, 1926, p. 277).

15 *Sensus spiritualis, ordinatus ad recte credendum, potest fundari in illo modo figurationis quo vetus testamentum significat novum; et sic est allegoricus sensus vel typicus, secundum quod ea quae in veteri testamento contingerunt,*

exponuntur de Christo et ecclesia; vel potest fundari in illo modo figurationis quo novum simul et vetus significant Ecclesiam triumphantem; et sic est sensus anagogicus (*Quodlibetal Question* 7, a. 15 (Mandonnet, p. 277).

16 *...quas male intellectas pro se inducebat* (*Expositio circa decretalem secundam...*, Mandonnet, *Opuscula...*, vol. 4, p.347).

17 Quoted in Henri de Lubac, *Exégèse médiévale*, vol.1, Paris: Aubier, 1959, p. 23.

Chapter 6
The Judgment of Bonaventure

Thomas Aquinas's clear and forceful opposition to Joachim could simply have been adopted by his Franciscan contemporary and colleague at the university of Paris, Bonaventure Fidanza, in order to destroy the memory of Joachim and the sequels of his theology. The problems that emerged from Joachimism, however, were not the same for the communities to which the two doctors belonged. In spite of the early enthusiasm of Humbert de Romans, the Friars preachers turned out to be more immune to the Joachimite virus than the Friars minor, among whom the virus spread far and wide. Bonaventure was as opposed to Joachim as Thomas Aquinas, but he chose another way of argumentation. His attempt to heal the Franciscan heart consisted both in demolishing the Joachimite constructions and in painting an alternative view of the future and of the eschaton that was closely linked to the traditional Trinitarian doctrine. His argumentation was also engaged, and critically so, in the problems that arose from the lenient position of Alexander IV toward Joachim.

*

Bonaventure was elected Minister general at the general chapter of the *Ara coeli*, in Rome, in February of 1257, with the mission to stop the Joachimite virus that was infecting the order. To that end it was necessary to uphold the memory of Francis as he was, and not as the Spirituals imagined him. It was equally necessary to encourage serious theological studies, since Joachim's analysis of history and his predictions departed from traditional theology, and Gherardo's interpretations veered still further away from the common tradition.

While, the chapter over, Giovanni da Parma retired to the solitude of Greccio, where, at Christmas of 1223, Francis had improvised a sort of nativity-play in which local people acted as participants and witnesses, Bonaventure tackled the serious problems he inherited.

The problems that touched the Friars minor directly were due both to Giovanni's tolerance of Gherardo da Borgo San Donnino's speculations on the nature and destiny of the Order, and to the apparent determination of the Holy See to protect the memory of Joachim. If this protection did not also cover Gherardo, it extended to Giovanni da Parma. Far from regarding the former Minister general as totally disgraced, Nicholas III (pope, 1277-1280), in 1279, sent him on a diplomatic mission to Basileus Michael VIII Palaeologos (emperor, 1259-1282). Giovanni died on the way, before he could embark for Greece. In the 1260's and 1270's, however, there was an additional and broader problems, of a philosophical and theological nature, in developments that were taking place in the faculty of Arts in Paris.

The expulsion of Guillaume de St-Amour from the kingdom of France,—when he simply retired in his own country of Franche-Comté[1],—had left the faculty of Arts without the guidance of one who, though vitriolic toward the Friars, remained traditional in his basic theological assumptions. Soon, however, there developed at the university a philosophical interpretation of Aristotle, inspired by Averroes (Ibn Roschd), which disregarded the Christian dogmas. Siger de Brabant (c.1235-c.1281) was its most prominent advocate. The official reaction came late, on 17 March 1277, with the condemnation by the bishop of Paris of 219 propositions, several of which were actually taken from the writings of Thomas Aquinas. The theologians, however, and notably Bonaventure, had long anticipated the condemnation of Averroism, and in particular the contention that the world is eternal. We will examine the problem at some length.

*

Already in his *Commentary on the Sentences* Bonaventure had criticized at length the arguments in favor of an eternal world[2]. What he found wrong with them was not the possibility of a world that would have no beginning and no end. It was primarily the affirmation that the world had to be eternal, and thus that the Creator was not really free to create as He willed. It was secondarily the mistake of admitting that the question whether the material universe is created from all eternity or in time cannot be answered at the level of philosophy, although it is certainly taught in the Christian faith. This position was actually that of Thomas Aquinas[3].

Bonaventure in fact implicitly admitted the conditional possibility of an eternal world. This is patent from his clear statement in the *Disputed Questions on the Mystery of the Trinity:*

> Granted that from eternity God intended to produce the world, because, however, he did not want the production of the world to be from eternity, but only in time, it follows that he produced it in time, without any mutation of his will; and the effect began, the cause having no beginning[4].

In the same vein Bonaventure wrote in his *Commentary on the Sentences* that if creation were by natural necessity it would be as eternal as the Creator himself, whereas creation by willed choice begins when God decides it must begin. God could have made creation eternal, but God decided otherwise, presumably because it would not have been entirely proper and congruous. A temporal creation is a better sign for us of the Creator's power and wisdom. Accordingly, "the divine will, which acts in keeping with wisdom, produced [the creature], not from eternity, but in time, since it disposed and willed as it acted[5]." Bonaventure went further. He granted that it would be philosophically more acceptable to think that God created the whole world, matter and form, from eternity, rather than matter only, as many of the Greeks thought, for it is in its hylomorphic integrity, as matter and form together, that the world is a shadow of the eternal God: "Thus it seems reasonable that the creatures, or the world, which is the shadow of the Supreme Light, be also eternal[6].» Believing that this was Aristotle's teaching, Bonaventure calls him "the most excellent among philosophers." It does not follow, however, that the creatures must be eternal. In fact, the notion of an eternal world entails a philosophical dilemma to which Bonaventure saw no solution: The number of created souls would eventually become infinite, and infinity cannot be an attribute of anything created. One could respond that a world without beginning does not mean a humanity without beginning, or that an endless humanity only posits an endlessly increasing, but always finite, number of souls. The theories, however, that try to avoid having an infinite number of souls in an eternal creation seemed to

Bonaventure esthetically and morally repulsive: For instance, the souls would eventually die; or a number of souls would undergo reincarnation; or there would be only one soul for all humanity, as in Averroism. Bonaventure concludes: "This error has a bad beginning and the worst possible end."

This critique of the idea of an eternal world is not unlike Thomas Aquinas's affirmation, in *Contra Gentes*, that the world in fact had a beginning: The Catholic faith "posits that nothing besides God has been always, but that everything has a beginning, except the one eternal God[7].» Thomas also held that creation in time makes better sense because it is more in harmony with the Creator's only possible purpose, which is to show the divine goodness at work in the divine works[8].

As it is organized and it lives its successive existence on earth, the Church, though eternally conceived in God's Word, is evidently part of the created order. Likewise, the eternal Word has, in the Incarnation, become a member of the human race and a sharer, be it the central one, in the natural order. It is therefore not out of place, in order to understand the Church and appreciate its beauty, to take a brief look at the inner structure of creation, as it was discussed among the scholastics in the thirteenth century, and notably by Thomas Aquinas and Bonaventure.

Aristotle's opinion was that matter has always been and the Creator or Demiurge only had to organize it by giving it a proper form. In this case the basic question regarded the eternity or temporality of creation. We have already noted that Bonaventure rejected the Aristotelian position. The biblical evidence was that God created the universe, so to say, in depth, that is, in its totality, matter as well as form, though this formula is not biblical language and the distinction between matter and form is not Hebraic, but Greek. The theologians expressed this insight by saying that the world was created *ex nihilo*, out of nothing. The creative act was such that the first moment of existence of the world was the first moment of time. As Augustine had written, the world was created *cum tempore*, along with time[9]. Temporal sequence belongs to the form of creaturely existence.

That creation was "from nothing" was equally affirmed by the angelic doctor and the seraphic doctor. They, however, understood it differently. Thomas admitted the partial validity of the philosophical argument for the eternity of the world, in that he considered mere reason to be unable to conclude with certainty whether the universe was created eternally or temporally. In other words, no one can be certain that time and the world in fact had a beginning, unless this is revealed by the Creator. Creation as such is nothing more than a relation of dependence of the creature on the Creator, who could well have willed such a relation to exist from all eternity, but in fact did not will it.

The position of the seraphic doctor is at the same time simpler and more complex. It is simpler in that it rests entirely on his understanding of *ex nihilo*. Creation *ex* or *de nihilo* implies that the creature has "being after non-being[10]," "after" having no chronological implications here. Creation in time is therefore a movement between the two moments of nothing and of being, the first of which, by definition, has no existence. The movement is thus *ex nihilo*. The Creator is at the same time utterly perfect and utterly simple. "Because most perfect, all perfections must be ascribed to Him; as most simple, these perfections posit no diversity in Him, and therefore no variation or change. Thus, while remaining stable, He gives motion to all things[11].» The ultimate objection to an eternal world is not merely philosophical. It flows from a viewing of the created images of God that occurs in the twilight between faith and philosophy. When, enlightened by faith, the believing mind reads the book of the world, it perceives "its origin, its course, and its end," which themselves point to the Creator's "power... providence... justice[12].» As Bonaventure wrote elsewhere: "See how the wisdom of God is hidden in natural philosophy[13].»

Thus it is that from the *Commentary on the Sentences* to the *In Hexaëmeron*, Bonaventure stated and restated that it is impossible for creation to be at the same time *ex nihilo* and without a beginning. The biblical doctrine of creation out of nothing, by the sole power of the Creator, thus acquires a metaphysical certainty that is denied by Thomas Aquinas. Though Bonaventure confesses that he is not quite certain of Aristotle's exact position, he tends to excuse the philosopher, because unacquainted with the biblical revelation, for affirming the eternity of the *materia prima* of the universe. Aristotle's excuse, as formulated in *In Hexaëmeron* VII, was that he "understood this as a philosopher speaking at the level of nature, namely, that it [the world] could not have a beginning from nature[14].» The Delorme formulation is clearer: "On Aristotle's opinion concerning the eternity of the world it may be said that he was right according to nature, but not absolutely (*simpliciter*), since everywhere he denies infinity[15].» Few scholars, however, have been puzzled by what, in Bonaventure's eyes, made Aristotle's opinion if not simply, at least relatively, correct. After I drew attention to this question in too short an article published in 1951, I was accused of completely misreading Bonaventure's doctrine[16]. My critic, however, identified neither the element of truth that Bonaventure found in Aristotle's erroneous doctrine of creation, nor the reason that prompted him to recognize this partial truth. Thus, the apparent variation between the *Disputed questions de Trinitate* and Bonaventure's other writings remained unexplained[17].

This was the crux of the matter in Bonaventure's objections to Averroism. His understanding of *ex nihilo* included a necessary beginning, the beginning of time, that Thomas Aquinas's definition did not include. In Thomas's understanding, time need have no beginning. Why this difference between the two doctors? Beyond the definition of terms, the two scholastics differed in their basic option regarding God. Thomas identified God primarily as Absolute Being, so that he saw the heavenly blessedness as a contemplation of the divine Essence. Bonaventure's perspective was more nuanced. In *Itinerarium* 3, the "primary Name" of God is indeed Being (*esse*), a Name revealed to Moses at the Burning Bush. It is symbolized by one of the two Cherubim on the Ark of the Covenant, who adore the mysteries of the divine Essence and its attributes (*essentialia Dei*). Being is as such the first "mode or degree" of the contemplation of God. In the New Testament, however, a new Name, *bonum*, the Good, designates God "principally and above all" *(principaliter et praecipue)*. This Name introduces a second "mode or degree" of contemplation of the "invisible and eternal" realities (*invisibilia et aeterna*), namely, the divine Persons and what is proper to each. If Being evokes the eternal Essence (the *ousia*) of God, the Good evokes the Three Persons. It is properly God's Trinitarian Name.

Now, in human experience the good should be freely chosen, or it is not really the best. Goodness implies will and freedom. As one then reflects on the Supreme Good, it appears that God is Supreme Will, Supreme Freedom. In fact, Franciscans in the fourteenth century will so focus on the Will of God that William of Ockham (c.1300- c.1350) will canonize the distinction, already made by John Duns Scotus (c.1265-1308), between the absolute scope of God's possibilities (*potentia absoluta*) and the chosen order of creation (*potentia ordinata*). In regard to creation this distinction implies that, in its actual order, creation includes a beginning that is necessary by virtue of the divine will. In the absolute order of what God could have done, however, nothing requires a temporal rather than an everlasting universe.

At this precise point the text to which I drew attention in 1951 makes perfect sense. Bonaventure distinguished between two aspects of an action. There is the decision to act, and act in such a way, and there is is the ensuing effect. The first aspect is interior and the second exterior. When God acts, the first aspect, interior to the Divinity, is eternal; the second aspect is external (*ad extra*) and temporal. The divine Will is eternally the proximate and immediate cause of the things to be produced, in their substance, disposition, and interior process; and their external reality is effective at the moment the divine Will, all-powerful and supremely free, has chosen. From all eternity God decided "to produce the world. And since God did not want the production of the world to be from eternity, but only in time, it was produced in time, no change having taken place in the will; and the effect began, the cause having no beginning[18].» Thus Bonaventure's reflection on eternity and time, God and the creature, anticipated some of the precisions and formulations that characterized the Franciscan school in the later Middle Ages. The vocabulary of Scotus or that of Ockham were not his vocabulary. An insight regarding the will of God that was similar to theirs, however, was already at work in his struggle with the philosophical views of the origin of the universe.

The philosophers made the mistaken assumption, or built the theory, that the world, or at least its matter, is eternal. This was Aristotle's error in the heyday of Greek philosophy. It was taken for granted in Neo-Platonism, for which the forms themselves proceed from the One by emanation and not by creation. It had been refuted in the sixth century, against Proclos, by the Christian philosopher Johannes Philoponos[19], an author with whom Bonaventure was not acquainted. The eternity of matter had been reaffirmed by Averroes, the distinguished Arab commentator on Aristotle. And the error recurred once again among the professors in the faculty of Arts of Paris, Bonaventure's contemporaries. This led them to find the Creator superfluous. And this denial of the Creator had lethal consequences beyond philosophy, for "to posit an eternal world is to upset the whole Scripture, and to say that the Son of God did not take flesh[20]. "

Philosophers have also theorized that all humans share one "intellect agent," the active instrument of knowledge in Aristotle's theory of cognition. In a sense, the theories of Siger de Brabant contained nothing new. They brought back to life Arabic philosophical notions that had been generally discarded in Christian thought. What was new was the relative success of these ideas, and the threat to the Christian faith that would materialize if they spread far and wide. The proposed theories would leave humans without individuality and liberty, and consequently without moral responsibility. In Bonaventure's words, "it amounts to saying that there is neither truth of faith nor salvation of souls or keeping of the commandments; and this is to say that the worst one is saved and the best one is damned." Criticism of the philosophers, a recurrent theme in Bonaventure's writings, remained a primary motivation for his last series of conferences at the Franciscan studium in Paris. It was not, however, in my judgment, the central topic of his three series of lectures.

As seen by Bonaventure, the theological question of Joachimism turned on three hinges: the possibility or non-possibility of an Eternal Gospel other than that of the Word made flesh, the Trinitarian reality of God, and the proper way to read Scripture. The possibility of a new and Eternal Gospel depended largely on the answers that were given to the other two questions. That the Holy Trinity is the transcendent and eternal model of the architectonic structures of creation, of the Church, and of the human soul was so evident in the Augustinian tradition that it was generally taken for granted. In this the Franciscan theologian fully agreed with his Dominican colleague. As he wrote,

> The first Table contains the commandments that relate us to God. God, however, is a Trinity, Father and Son and Holy Spirit. To the Father majesty is attributed, to the Son truth, and to the Holy Spirit goodness. Supreme Majesty is to be adored in the Father; Supreme Truth is to be faithfully affirmed in the Son; Supreme Goodness is to be sincerely loved in the Holy Spirit[21].

What follows from the Trinitarian principle, however, depends on the way the principle is understood and applied. Precisely, the Trinitarian theology of Bonaventure was extremely elaborate. On the matter of the marks of the Trinity in creation the theologians had two models at their disposal, the old one of Dionysius and the recent one of Joachim. It was relatively easy to show that the Joachimite model was at variance with the tradition. In the matter of reading Scripture, Bonaventure had elegantly outlined his principles in the prologue to his short *summa*, the *Breviloquium*. Particularly relevant to an enlightened reading of Scripture was his description of its *profunditas*. The depth of Scripture consists in a "multiplicity of mystical senses and understandings[22]," namely, «allegory..., tropology..., anagogy...» Allegory shows the Christian faith in the letter of Scripture. Tropology shows how believers should apply this faith in their life. Anagogy, or *sursum ductio* ("upward guidance") shows what they should hope for, namely, "the eternal happiness of the Blessed." In other words, the theological virtues of faith, love, and hope open up the spiritual meanings of the Scriptures as God's word in them is lived in the human soul. By the same token they are the key to the understanding of the universe. God's dominion and governance of the universe, and the admirable benevolence that is at work in salvation, are the basis of the natural Law. As he refers to *lex naturae*[4], Bonaventure not only explains the Mosaic revelation, tied to the Law of nature; he also sees the first three commandments in their intimate links to the divine Trinity, that are known by revelation only. The whole purpose of the Law of nature, and of nature itself, is to serve God's self-revelation. "The understanding of God's commandments" occurs after "the ascent of the mountain," that is, symbolically, at "the summit of mind," *eminentia mentis*, that has received "the imprint of the eternal light[23]." Thus is nature itself radically dependent on God's creative relation to it.

As creaturely being relies on the divine Being who continuously creates it, so does human knowledge depend on a light that comes from God as the ultimate Truth. Here Bonaventure follows the Augustinian doctrine of illumination. The divine Word, *lumen de lumine* as in the Nicene-Constantinopolitan creed, makes himself the light of the minds in order that both angels and humans may have access to the certainty of true knowledge. In the soul's internal structure this is its highest point, *apex mentis*, which, aware of it or not, receives light from the Word of God. In the moral perspective of a fundamental conviction that the good exists, and that even in the midst of sin the soul feels an unquenchable desire for it, Bonaventure's Commentary on the Sentences identified this high point with *synderesis*, the high level of the soul that is never wrong and never fails[24]. Neither original sin nor actual sin has any effect on it. The sinful propensity of nature is never total. God's purity reaches the sinner even in the midst of willed evil.

On the one hand, Bonaventure holds that a natural knowledge of God is inscribed in the heart. On the other hand, grace is channeled through the Savior. It follows that the believers have two avenues toward God: "These two, the knowledge of the Creator and that of the Redeemer (*reparator*)... are the foundations of our faith[25]." There are, by implication, "two rays or two spiritual eyes that lead us in the way of the commands of God." Meanwhile, since the Creator is Three divine Persons who are jointly involved in the radiation of the divine light, there must be six modes of justice, that constitute so many ways to God. The primary justice relates directly to God. It is expressed in three commandments, each of which can be seen from the two points of view of creation and salvation. The second justice relates to God by way of the neighbor. Benevolence is implicit in the fourth commandment, in keeping with which the proper relation to God flowers in personal participation in the peace of the Sabbath; and it is explicit in the fifth. Innocence corresponds to the five remaining commandments. The following diagram sums it up:

—Before God	First justice, express in 3 precepts	
as Being and Creator of being	–Father	1st precept
	–Son	2nd precept
	–Spirit	3rd precept

as Redeeming and Giver of grace	–Father	1st precept
	–Son	2nd precept
	–Spirit	3rd precept

—Before the neighbor	Second justice, expressed in 7 precepts
benevolence	–two affirmative precepts: 4th and 5th
innocence	–six negative precepts: 6th to 10th

This analysis of the ten commandments has a sharp anti-Joachimite edge that may well escape the casual reader. For, if each of the first three commandments honors one divine Person in particular, their observance is evidently not successive. All the commandments of God are valid at all times and must be observed simultaneously, in keeping with the Three Persons' unanimous action. This, however, is in direct contradiction of what Joachim claimed to be the specific revelations coming successively from each of the Three, in the Old, the New, and the Eternal Gospels.

*

The *Lectures on the Seven Gifts of the Holy Spirit* were given during Lent of 1268. They rounded up the picture outlined in the *Lectures on the Ten Commandments.* Taken together, the two series presuppose a close correlation between creation and redemption. As was the case with the first series, the allusions to contemporaries were not blatant. They nevertheless were clear as they pointed to contradictions between philosophical conceptions and the doctrine of grace. Grace is given only by God, and its nature is easily gathered from the biblical revelation. The gifts of the Spirit are received in baptism and they equip the baptized for growth and perfection in faith. As such they are instruments of the return of human creatures to the Creator's original purpose. The immediate fruits of baptismal regeneration, they are destined in turn to bear additional fruits which, in the symbolic language that Bonaventure liked to use, should eventually adorn the twelve trees of the soul's paradise.

The Franciscan school generally held that Adam and Eve were not created in a state of sanctifying grace, but in a state of natural innocence. Since they were aware of God's will regarding the Garden of

Eden, and the commandments were imprinted in their heart, the first humans could have remained in happy innocence with the help of what Bonaventure called *gratia gratis data*, grace graciously given in view of specific actions. This notion of grace will eventually give way to the concept of actual grace of later theology, when it will have the task of drawing sinful humanity away from sin and toward God. In the lectures of 1268, however, as already in Bonaventure's *Commentary on the Sentences*, *gratia gratis data* is more enabling and strengthening than remedial.

*

It was in the series of 1273, *On the Six Days of Creation,* that Bonaventure fully formulated his doctrinal opposition to Joachim's spiritual and ecclesial conceptions.

One may find a symbolic indication of their character in the fact that they were not given in Lent, but in the Paschal time. While the observance of the Commandments is propedeutic, and the appropriation of the baptismal gifts is initiatory, the celebration of the resurrection of Christ on Easter Sunday opens the gate that leads to the fullness of grace and to heavenly glory. The six days of creation, as analyzed, unveil the spiritual dimension of the created world and, through the toils of the Church militant, its fulfillment in the Church triumphant. Where Joachim had sought for a historical transformation of the Gospel in application of his hermeneutical method of *concordia*, Bonaventure shows how the present status of the Church leads the faithful to their heavenly home, of which they may obtain a foretaste in their own spiritual ascent. Though Joachim is never mentioned in the lectures, his speculations act as a foil against which the lecturer is silently testing his doctrines.

Bonaventure's central argument is given in Lecture XXI. It is taken from what must be said of the highest creatures that are known in the Judeo-Christian tradition, the angels, considered in the Dionysian perspective that was familiar to medieval theologians: Since a multiform reference to the Holy Trinity is true of the being of angels, all the more will the inferior creatures that we are depend on the Trinity in their very essence and person. In the Dionysian perspective, each hierarchy spreads the light it has received and illumines the next lower hierarchy, which in turn receives this light to the extent it is able. "Note that the first hierarchy neither originates in, nor is illumined by, any one but God; the middle one is illumined by God and by the highest one; the lowest is illumined by God and by the highest and by the middle one; the ecclesial hierarchy is illumined by all of them[26]." The Church's hierarchy therefore belongs to the lowest level. It exists in the context of humankind, and their position among the created hierarchies makes human beings far inferior to the lowest angels.

This is not unlike, one may note today, the physical location of the human race on what is only "a medium-sized planet orbiting around an average star in the outer suburbs of an ordinary spiral galaxy, which is itself only one of about a million million galaxies in the observable universe[27]," to say nothing of layers of the universe that may not be observable, or of other hypothetical universes structured with different dimensions, as in non-Euclidian geometry, in other spaces and times than ours.

*

In order to go the heart of the theological opposition to Joachim after the decade of the 1260's failed to bring about the revelation of the Eternal Gospel, our next two chapters will study how Bonaventure presented the contemplative nature of the Church in his *Lectures on the Six Days of Creation.*

Notes

1 Franche-Comté was incorporated in the kingdom of France in 1678 (Peace of Nijmegen).

2 *Commentary on the Sentences,* II, d. 1, p. 1, a. 1, q. 2.

3 S. Th. I q. 46, a.2.

4 *Et hoc habet divina voluntas, quia simul est omnipotentissima et liberrima; et ideo, licet ab aeterno voluerit producere mundum, quia tamen non voluit productionem mundi esse ab aeterno, sed solum in tempore, hinc est quod in tempore produxit, nulla facta mutatione in voluntate, et incepit effectus, non incipiente causa* (*De Trinitate*, q. 6, a. 1, ad 15).

5 C. S. II, d.1, p. 1, a. 1, q. 2, ad 6.

6 C. S. II, d. 1, p. 1, a. 1, q. 2, corpus.

7 *Contra Gentes* II, ch. 34.

[8] *Finis divinae voluntatis in rerum productione est ejus bonitas in quantum per causata manifestatur* (C. G., II, ch. 38, ad 6).

[9] *De Civitate Dei*, XI, vi (*Bibliothèque Augustinienne. La Cité de Dieu, xi-xiv*, Paris: Desclée de Brouwer, 1959, p. 50).

[10] *Breviloquium*, part II, ch. 1, n. 3.

[11] C. S., II, d. 1, p. 1, a. 6, q. 1, ad 6.

[12] *Itinerarium mentis in Deum,* ch. 1, n. 12.

[13] *De Reductione artium ad theologiam*, n. 22.

[14] *Intellexit hoc ut philosophus, loquens ut naturalis, scilicet quod per naturam non potuit incipere* (*In Hexaëmeron*, VII, 2).

[15] *De sensu tamen Aristotelis de mundi aeternitate potest dici quod secundum naturam verum sensit, non simpliciter, quia ubique infinitatem reprobat* (Delorme, p. 99).

[16] Fernand Van Steernbergen, "*Saint Bonaventure contre l'éternité du monde*" (Guy Bougerol, ed., *S. Bonaventura. 1274-1074,* Grottaferrata: Collegio San Bonaventura, 1973, vol. 3, p. 258-278).

[17] As Van Steernbergen denied the variation, he also misunderstood the crucial text of the *Disputed Question de Trinitate: nisi pro eo tempore quo vult* does not mean, «*seulement pour la durée temporelle qu'elle a voulu lui assigner*» (p. 262): «except for the time duration it has wanted to assign to it»; it means: «except for the moment He chose.» The question is beginning, not duration.

[18] See above, note 4.

[19] Colin E. Gunton, *The Triune Creator. A Historical and Systematic Study*, Grand Rapids: Eerdmans, 1998, p. 95-96.

[20] *In Hexaëmeron*, II, 24.

[21] *In Decem Praeceptis*, I, 22.

[22] *Breviloquium,* prologue, §4, n.1.

[23] *In Decem Praeceptis*, II, 2.

[24] Tavard, *Transiency...*, p. 97-100.

[25] *In Decem Praeceptis*, II, 9.

[26] *In Hexaëmeron*, XXI, 21.

[27] Stephen W. Hawking, *A Brief History of Time. From the Big Bang to Black Holes,* Toronto: Bantam Books, 1988, p. 126.

Chapter 7
The Hierarchies

The popes who protected the memory of Joachim may have feared some imminent event that would justify his prophecies. Essentially, Joachim had prophesied a total transformation of the present Church into a contemplative Church. But what could such a Church be? If the ecclesial structure on earth has abiding validity beyond the present moment, the fully contemplative Church can only be the Church in heaven. Precisely, the high point in Bonaventure's struggle with the legacy from Joachim was his description of the heavenly Church. Because the medieval theory of angels closely reflected the doctrine of the Trinity, angelology offered a vantage point from which one could show the Church's essentially Trinitarian dimension even in the earthly conditions of the Church militant.

*

The angels of the Old Testament may owe some of their features to Persian conceptions that the exiles may have known in Babylon. They nevertheless are an integral feature of the biblical horizon. In a scene that became popular in Byzantine piety and art, the Pentateuch shows three angels visiting Abraham (Gen. 18, 1-15). The prophetic books frequently mention "the Angel of the Lord." In the New Testament the Archangel Gabriel is the agent of the Annunciation to Mary. Neither Testament, however, discusses the nature of angels, their type of motion, or their mode of cognition, questions that interested medieval theologians to a surprising extent. Thomas Aquinas researched the nature, cognition, movements, and functions of angels in no less than fifteen questions of the *Summa theologiae* (I q. 50 to 65, the last two discussing the fallen angels). In his *Commentary on the Sentences*, bk II, Bonaventure also speculated on the nature of angels (d. II; III, part I), their creation (d. III), their mode of cognition and of affection (d. III, p.II, a.2;3), their hierarchy (d. IX), and the missions on which they may be sent by the Creator (d. X; XI). These prolonged reflections on the angelic nature were largely prompted by the familiarity of the scholastics with the angelology of St. Paul[1], amplified by Dionysius, that had come to them through the theologians of the Carolingian age, notably the abbot of St. Dionysius, near Paris, Hilduin, and the Platonist John Scot Eriugena, who both had translated the works of Dionysius.

As the sun is powerful, resplendent, and hot, so is "the Father supremely powerful, the Son supremely beautiful, the Spirit supremely burning... And as these three, power, splendor, and heat, are one sun, so are the Father, the Son, and the Spirit one God[2]." Each Person enlightens the believer by virtue of its own personhood and by its eternal and simultaneous dwelling in the other two. The Trinity thus shines with nine eternal lights that are reflected in the nine choirs of angels, which, in turn, radiate with them. The highest three are the image of the First Person. The Seraphim experience and point to the Father in himself; the Cherubim experience and point to the Father indwelling the Son; the Thrones experience and point to the Father indwelling the Spirit. The next three Lights shine in the intermediate choirs (Virtues, Powers, Dominations). They reflect the Word in Self, in the Father, and in the Spirit. The last three Lights, reflecting the Spirit in Self, in the Word, and in the Father, illumine the lowest angelic level (Principalities, Archangels, Angels). Like the columns of gothic architecture, which trace a multitude of lines as they ascend to one point at the summit of the vault, the angelic choirs point to the Divine Trinity in a dynamic and multiform style. Angels do not draw attention to themselves. They always point to a divine Person, and thereby to the Three. Thus the angelic choirs form "a divine order, knowledge, and action assimilated to deiformity as far as is possible, and proportionally ascending in the likeness of God toward the divine illuminations communicated to it[3]." They constitute a scale of spiritual creatures that differ from one another by the mode and extent of their deiformity. God alone illumines the highest order; God and the first order illumine the second; God and the first two orders illumine the third. And the ecclesial hierarchy, at the foot of the scale, receives light from God and from all the choirs of angels.

This view of the angelic universe ruins the perspective of Joachim, for it shows the presence and influence of the Three Persons as being essentially simultaneous, and not, as Joachim imagined, tied to the on-going march of the world. As it reveals a world of spiritual creatures that is normally invisible to human eyes, it also offers a key to the esthetic aspects of creation and of the Church. In the Dionysian scheme the multiform Trinitarian reference of angels is passed on to the next lower hierarchy, which receives it to the extent of its capacity. At the bottom of the process it is passed to the Church on earth: "Note that the first hierarchy neither originates in, nor is illumined by, any one but God; the middle one is illumined by God and by the highest one; the lowest is illumined by God and by the highest and by the middle one; the ecclesial hierarchy is illumined by all of them[4]."

*

There undoubtedly is an infinite ocean of divine attributes, most of which are unknown, and presumably unknowable, to inferior intelligences. Each one of those we know can be contemplated in those nine exemplifications of the divine presence. As originating principle, the Father is the "power, wisdom, and will" that are shown in the law of nature. Present in the mediating Son, He is the "piety, truth, and holiness" that are shown in the law of Scripture[5]. The Latin word, *pietas*, connotes the loving relationship between parents and children, and by the same token God's loving attitude to the creatures and the return of this love from the creatures before God. Present in the Spirit, the Father is the ultimate Source of grace and holiness. Nature therefore proclaims the law of piety, Scripture the law of truth, and Grace the law of sanctity. Taken together, the three laws show the Father, the Son, and the Spirit as "pious, true, and holy, giving the pious law of Nature, the true law of Scripture, the holy law of Grace[6]." Since the commandments derive from God's governing authority, they number, not surprisingly, nine plus one: "The ninefoldness is completed and perfected by the addition of oneness[7]." That is, the nine are brought to perfection in love.

God is the source of all blessedness, the originating model of which is provided by the attributes of *aeternitas, formositas, jucunditas*, "eternity in the Father, beauty in the Son, joy in their mutual Link[8]." Each of these again initiates a triple contemplation, since each Person may be sought in itself and as it dwells in the other two: "Authority is proper to the Son as He is in the Father, virility as He is in himself, victory as He is in the Spirit[9]." Again, because beatitude relates to knowledge and love, to instruction and education, it "nurtures in supreme sweetness" by virtue of its three faces: certitude in leading, wisdom in teaching, zeal in preserving. "And thus the Spirit, as being in the Father, leads; as being in the Son, teaches; as being in Self, preserves[10]." In the solar symbolism, "all celestial and subcelestial spirits look to the Sun. In these nine ways the creature is assimilated, as far as is possible, to the Creator." That nine aspects of the Godhead are thus offered to the believers' contemplation is evidently incompatible with the belief that the Old Testament was rendered obsolete by the New, and that the New will soon give way to the Spirit's Eternal Gospel. "All hierarchy corresponds to the Father and the Son and the Holy Spirit [11]." This reflects the permanent relevance of each of the Three Persons, and their constant and equal influence on all creatures.

That Joachim's methodological principles are incompatible with the Catholic teaching on the Three Persons is further brought out by reflection on *monarchia*, the divine "Monarchy". The one God is the source of all else that is, and thereby the Lord and Master of all creatures. This is a philosophical implication of monotheism. In addition, the more theological meaning of the term derives from the time, in the third century, when Tertullian refuted the modalist doctrines of Praxeas. Here, Monarchy implies authority, because it first denotes authorship, the initiating capability of the Source of all. Because the First Person is the only source of the Word and of the Spirit, one may speak of the Monarchy of the First Person over the Second and the Third. The Monarchy of the First guarantees the equality of the Three, as was affirmed equivalently in the Creed of Nicaea-Constantinople: *Credo in unum Deum, Patrem omnipotentem*... It derives from the Father's "fontal fullness[12]." The doctrine of the Monarchy is presupposed by the liturgy as perfect worship. As Bonaventure says it in an untranslatable phrase: "It is necessary to the perfect worship of God to think and to believe that God is *principium aeternaliter principians principiantem.*[13]" Let us say, "an initiation eternally initiating an initiator." That God is eternally fruitful is evident to those who think of God *altissime et piissime* ("most highly and most piously[14]"). Being "from no one," unproduced and ungenerated, the Father is the sole origin of all that is. In an unusually irenic side-remark Bonaventure notes: "In this Christians, Jews, Muslims, and even heretics are in agreement[15]."

In the classical painting of the angels' visit to Abraham,—both in Byzantine iconography and in Western art,—the Three Persons appeared to Abraham disguised as angels. The two who later made their way to Sodom were "the Son and the Spirit, who were sent by the Father; and therefore the Father did not appear there [in Sodom], though he appeared among the Three, for the Father appeared but is never sent[16]." The Word of God bears witness to the Father's Monarchy: "The Word expresses the Father as the principle which produces by itself (*de se*), thus explaining and showing the production of the Holy Spirit and his own, that is, the production of Eternal Realities[17]." The vision of the fourth day of creation suggests a threefold contemplation: "Unless there be reflection of the highest Monarchy, contuition of the descent of the Church militant therefrom, and hierarchic adornment of itself, [the soul] will never be contemplative[18]." When these conditions are met, the soul is open to God's gifts, and it receives "the contemplation of itself, of the Church militant, and of the heavenly Monarchy[19]."

*

This sort of reflection makes ecclesiology a dimension of angelology. Medieval theologians rarely discussed the Church's nature, function, and structure, for the Church was taken for granted in the structure of European society, that hinged around the two poles of Pope and Emperor. It was in fact the emergence of heresies that prompted reflection on the nature and structure of the Church. Toward the middle of the twelfth century Hugh of Rouen (c.1080-1164), reacting against the anti-institutional tenets of a new sect in Britany, composed what seems to be the first treatise on the Church: *Contra haereticos sui temporis, seu De Ecclesia et ministris ejus libri tres.*

Despite the absence of discrete ecclesiological tractates before the papal schism in the fourteenth century[20], two points may be affirmed.

Firstly, an ecclesiology is necessarily implied in the Christian belief in God-given sacraments. Even when, toward the end of the twelfth century, the sacraments were universally limited to seven holy actions, sacramental theology required ministers to administer them. The sacraments therefore evoked the Church's hierarchical structure. Secondly, following the Dionysian tradition, reflection on the Church was inseparable from reflection on the presence of the Holy Trinity in the heart of the faithful. The Church provided the Christian people with the Scriptures, the sacraments, the creeds, the proclamation and explanation of the word of God. When Hugh of St. Victor (c.1096-1141) identified the dedication of church buildings as the first sacrament, he did so because a church building is the normal setting for sacramental celebrations. The building in turn reflects the sacred dimension of the Church.

Another approach to ecclesiology featured the apocalyptic vision of the Woman in heaven: "A great portent appeared in the sky: a Woman clothed with the sun, with the moon under her feet, and on her head a crown of twelve stars" (Apo. 12,1). That the Woman in the sky is sun-clad evidently implies that, despite the conventions of Christian iconography, she is nude. The sunlight bathes her from all sides and is faithfully reflected by her. She stands on the moon, not, as often depicted, on a crescent, but on the full lunar orb. She is clothed in a triple light since she is bathed in light from below, illumined on all sides by the rays of the sun, and a twelve-star diadem throws more light on her from above. Understood metaphorically, the sun is the heavenly Monarchy, "a life-giving, luminous, warming Sun, from which nine lights arise in the soul, the lights of divine Excellence, of divine Influence, and of divine Presidency[21]," each of which sends out three beams. The solar light is the Holy Trinity centered on the Monarchy of the First Person. The nine lights are divine attributes that are manifest in God's relation with the Woman. And the Woman is "the contemplative soul," supported by "the Church militant." This grounding position of the Church, which ensures stability to the soul, denotes strength. Just as the moon receives its light from the sun, so does "the Church militant from the heavenly Jerusalem ..., our Mother, for she is the mother of the graces (*influentiae*) by which we are made children of God[22]." The Church militant was previously defined as

> a gathering of rational beings,... a union of rational beings who live in concord and uniformity, through a concordant and uniform keeping of divine Law, through a concordant and uniform cohesion of divine peace, through a concordant and uniform harmony of divine praise[23].

This is evidently another kind of *concordia* than that of Joachim. It is not a literal correspondence between the Old Testament, the New Testament, and the Eternal Gospel, but the conformity with God that derives from following the divine Law, the union of hearts that flows from heavenly peace, and the spiritual unity that is experienced in the liturgical sacrifice of praise. In this setting the apocalyptic image of the Woman acquires a special significance. This may be seen by looking at the introductions to the lectures. The first three open on *Ecclesiasticus* 1, 5: *In medio ecclesiae*... ("In the middle of the Church he opened his mouth..."). Lectures IV to VII open on Genesis 1,4: *Vidit Deus lucem quod esset bonum*... ("God saw the light, and it was good..."). The next three, VIII to X, start with Genesis 1,8: *Vocavit Deus firmamentum coelum*... ("God called the firmament, sky..."). This is followed by Corinthians 3, 18, where Paul tells the Christians that they should "reflect the Lord's glory,... going from light to light...," an eschatological perspective that dominates XI and XII. Lectures XIII to XIX are then opened by Genesis 1,9-12: *Congregentur aquae*..., the gathering of the waters into seas marking the origin of germination and the creation of life. With Lectures XX, XXI, and XXIII the perspective changes, as it is now focussed on the emergence of the sun and the moon in Genesis 1,16: *Fecit Deus duo luminaria magna*... It is within this meditation on the Light of the Sun and its reflection by the moon that the vision of the Woman in the sky,—Lecture XXII,—is placed.

This sequence of biblical texts illustrates a spiritual process. The word proclaimed in the *ecclesia* (I-III) leads to the creation of light (IV-VII), and hence to contemplation of the sky as the image of heaven (VIII-X). Passing next from its location outside and above the faithful to an interior setting in the soul, heaven becomes the inner torch of an interior journey to deeper and brighter lights (XI-XII). In this process the mind (*mens*, the soul in its intellectual capacities) is transformed. It becomes "intelligence taught by Scripture" (*intelligentia per Scripturam erudita*), where it learns about God's marvelous works (XIII-XIX). Finding itself enabled to contemplate these works, the soul becomes "intelligence caught up in contemplation" (*intelligentia per contemplationem suspensa*), when it receives the ultimate illumination from the Sun, the moon, and the stars. This final enlightenment (XX-XXI; XXIII) provides the vital context for the vision of the Woman in heaven (XXII). The Church then appears as the gathering of the faithful who are equipped for life by being part of this gathering. The soul lives and is nurtured in the Church. Conversely the Church/Moon serves the soul, now identified as the Sun-clad Woman, who, naked before God, is bathed in the divine attributes. There thus develops a dynamic ecclesiology of progressive interiority and spirituality. The Church militant has a single purpose: to serve the contemplative soul, so that, clothed in the divine Light, the soul can be God's ultimate dwelling-place. This ecclesial status of the soul is the fruit of the higher gifts of strength, counsel, intelligence, and wisdom. The starting-point of the human pilgrimage being the visibly external Church, the end is interiority, which is included in ecclesiality like the purpose of an action in its beginning. Genesis leads to, and includes, the Apocalypse. The struggles of the soul take place in the horizon of a union with God which, already actualized in baptism, reaches awareness in adult life and fullness at the eschaton. The spiritual Church that is interior to the soul can in turn act as a guide to the institution of the Church militant: "The heavenly hierarchy illustrates the Church militant[24]." The magisterial hierarchy is therefore seen by Bonaventure on the model of the angelic hierarchy. The ecclesial world duplicates the angelic world at a lower level:

> The Church militant in its history (*processus*) has three basic orders, corresponding to the supreme hierarchy, three progressive orders, corresponding to the intermediate hierarchy, three perfective (*consummantes*) orders, corresponding to the lowest hierarchy. The basic ones correspond to the highest, for in the spiritual realm the foundations are on high[25] (*fundamenta sunt altissima*).

The basic orders express the divine Fatherhood, the progressive orders Sonship, the perfective orders Spirithood. In a sense the basic orders correspond to the Patriachs with the stability of their faith, and further to the angelic Thrones and what they evoke of God, namely, the Father in Self. The Prophets with the clarity of their knowledge reflect the Cherubim and ultimately the Father dwelling in the Son. The Apostles correspond to the Father indwelling the Spirit. In the progressive orders the Martyrs show the Eternal Son dwelling in the Father; the Confessors show the Son in himself; and the Virgins show the Son indwelling the Spirit. The perfective order of the Apostles, who burn with the fervor of charity, reflects the Seraphim and, in God, the Father himself. In the Church this order includes, firstly, "prelates who have authority," the bishops, secondly, professors "of philosophy, law, theology, or whatever good art serves the good of the Church," thirdly, the religious. Bishops point to the Spirit dwelling in the Father, professors to the Spirit dwelling in the Son; and religious, practitioners of the monastic life, "are the last, since the world must be consummated in chastity, for the last do not generate offspring[26]." In the angelic world they correspond respectively to Principalities, Archangels, and Angels.

This imaging of the Holy Trinity and the angels takes the Church and its hierarchy beyond all static models. The Church is radically spiritual, open to, and reflective of, the infinite abundance of divine mercies. Like Scripture itself the Church is multiform and omniform. The hierarchic orders correspond also to the "three ways" of purgation, illumination, and perfection that medieval spirituality had inherited from Dionysius. As Bonaventure advised the abbess of the Poor Clares of Longchamp (probably Blessed Isabel, sister of the saintly king Louis IX): "If you desire to be raised to the second and the third heaven, go through the first, which is your heart[27]." The purgative way ascends from self-knowledge as one struggles with impurities, ignorance, and demonic temptations[28]. At the institutional level, purification defines the purpose of porters, who, like Angels, exclude the undesirable[29], lectors, who, like Archangels, exercise the teaching office in their liturgical functions, and exorcists, who, like Principalities, fight devils and demons.

The illuminative way winds through a sequence of Spirit-given insights into the depths of self and of the divine revelation. It is symbolized by Acolytes, who carry the lights and prepare the cruets, Subdeacons, who read the epistle and prepare the chalice, and Levites

(Deacons), who read the gospel and bring the chalice to the celebrant. Like the angels at Bethlehem the deacons should announce joy to the people, for the gospel they proclaim radiates with "the chief light that enlightens every human who comes into this world[30]." The angelic models of this middle ecclesial order are Powers, Virtues, and Dominations.

In the perfective way the soul begins to taste and see the tenderness of God. This is represented institutionally by the sacerdotal, episcopal, and patriarchal degrees of the hierarchy. The sacerdotal function leads the faithful to perfection (*consummatio*) through the sacraments, "without which there is no salvation[31]." The higher authority of bishops, patriarchs, and the pope adds nothing to their sacramental character, for there is no higher degree (*gradus*) than the priesthood received in ordination.[32] The three levels of the ordained are parallel to the Thrones (priests, who receive the fullness of *sacerdotium*), the Cherubim (bishops, "who must know the Scriptures"), and the Seraphim (patriarchs, entrusted with "eminence and power"). "The pope," Bonaventure adds, "should be the most perfect of all. If thus the internal order tallied with the external, it would be the best." The external scale of authority should never stray far from the spiritual model of the Three Ways. The exercises of the spiritual life,—action, repose, and a union of action and repose,—open a complementary view of the hierarchy: The laity lead the active life; prelates or clerics lead a mixed life, contemplation and action; at the highest level stand the contemplatives, or monks.[33]

The fluency of this pattern is striking. At the summit of the hierarchy, directly turned to the divine as such, the contemplatives are spread over three groups as Suppliants, Scholars, and Mystics, these last being practitioners of *modus sursumactivus* (the "ascent-active" mode[34]). The suppliants, "totally given to prayer, devotion, and the praise of God" except when occupied by manual labor, are the "black and white monks" of medieval society, that is, the Benedictines in their black habit and, wearing white, "the Cistercians, Premonstratensians, Carthusians, the Order of Grandmont, and Canons regular." The Fiorensians are not listed, though they were still flourishing in the early 1270's, and wearing a white habit like the Cistercians. Even if one can argue that the Order of Fiore is included in the reference to white monks, it is hardly due to an oversight that it is not mentioned by name.

As to the scholars, who devote their life to the study of Scripture, "which is not understood except by souls that are pure[35]," they are identified as the Friars preachers and Friars minor, Dominicans and Franciscans. Some among them seek scholarship first and unction second; others do the reverse. The Scholars belong to the Cherubinic order. Finally, the Seraphic order, the highest of all, devoted to *modus sursumactivus*, is, so far, reduced to St. Francis. "The third order [among the contemplatives] is that of those who rest in God according to *modum sursumactivum*, that is, in ecstasy or rapture[36]." The contradiction of Joachimism is implicit in the placement of the Franciscans among the Scholars, in the coexistence of the Seraphim with the Cherubim, the Thrones, and the other angelic choirs. For at this point no monastic age can replace or transform the clerical age. That Francis of Assisi, between the cliffs of La Verna, experienced rapture even before he chose a religious habit, confirms the anti-Joachimite bias of this perspective. If the Seraphic Order has existed on earth, this was only for a short time and it no longer exists outside of heaven.

There of course lurks a danger in aiming too high: "In hyperaction (*sursumactio*) there is the greatest difficulty, for the whole body is weakened, and unless the consolation of the Spirit was present it would not bear it." This is the highest level of contemplation. And, as Bonaventure continues, "here the Church will come to perfection" (*Et in his consummabitur Ecclesia*). The greatest mystics, who are "near to Jerusalem and have nothing to do but fly to it," will not be manifested before the eschaton: "This Order will not flourish unless Christ appears and suffers in his mystical body." It will be the true Seraphic Order, to which already St. Francis belonged. Since it will not appear before the return of Christ, its emergence will mark the end of history. At this point the Delorme version adds a reference to the divine Monarchy that deserves to be cited: "One is the Monarch, who is the principle of all orders and grades. The whole body of the Church is one, having one food, expecting one reward; it is such a beautiful Dove, as has been said, similar to the Moon. There is no member of Christ outside of this unity[37]." Thus the multiplicity of Orders in the Church and the flexibility of its hierarchies do not detract from its profound oneness, any more than the Trinity of divine Persons destroys the Unity of the divine Essence.

In other words, Joachim's prophecies are not to be trusted. And a warning is given to the clerical and the monastic levels of the Church: "Thus the Orders are distinguished according to their greater or lesser perfection. Yet the comparison is between ways of life (*status*), not between persons, for a lay person is sometimes more perfect than a religious[38]". The institutions of the Church militant are neither the whole nor the most important section of the Church. On earth it is ultimately the faithful soul that is the spiritual *Ecclesia*.

*

The ecclesiology of the Church militant that emerges from the contemplation of the Woman clothed with the sun is clearly based on the Dionysian notion of hierarchy. As it is applied to the Church's structure, however, this notion is plural, not singular. There is not only, as the Counter-Reformation will like to think, one hierarchy, identified with the magisterium, and narrowly restricted to the episcopal Order. The medieval view of the *Ecclesia* was generally fuller and more generous. The hierarchy includes the laity no less than the ordained, scholars no less than administrators and pastors. While it is architectonically a fine construction, this complex ecclesial structure has no meaning in itself. It derives its value from the heavenly model of the angelic world and, beyond, the eternal model of the Holy Trinity. The structure is visible, since one can identify a layperson, a scholar, and an ordained minister[39]. These distinctions, however, are not absolute: A religious can be ordained, and a lay person can be a religious. Moreover, a bishop has no advantage over anyone at the level of scholarship and the ability to teach. While the community results from the mutual enrichment of all the ecclesial Orders it finds its true sense at a more interior level that remains invisible, hidden in the faithful soul, *anima hierarchisata*, "the hierarchized soul[40]," or *mens animae hierarchisatae*, "the mind of the hierarchized soul." In the final analysis it is the believing soul that is, whatever the historical period, the spiritual Church. No other one is to be expected short of the eschaton.

Notes

1 See Rom. 8,38 (Virtues, Principalities), 1 Cor. 15,24 (Powers), Col. 1,16 (Dominations, Thrones).
2 *In Hexaëmeron* XXI, 2 (*Obras...*, BAC, p. 582).
3 *In Hexaëmeron* XXI, 17 (BAC, p. 592).
4 *In Hexaëmeron* XXI, 21 (BAC, p. 594-596).
5 "Piety is seen to inhere in every nature, even in insensible nature" (XXI, 6: BAC, p. 584).
6 XXI, 7 (BAC, p.584).
7 *Novenarius completur et perficitur per additionem unitatis* (XXI, 10: BAC, p. 586).
8 XXI, 23 (BAC, p. 596).
9 XXI, 14 (BAC, p. 590).
10 XXI, 15 (BAC, p. 590).
11 XXI, 20 (BAC, p. 594).
12 *Fontalis plenitudo* (C.S., I d. 2, a. un., q. 3; *Breviloquium* I, ch. 3, n. 7).
13 *Disputed Questions de Trinitate*, q.1, a.2, ad 11.
14 *D. Q. de Trinitate,* q.1 a.2.
15 *Et in hoc concordant Christiani, Judaei, et Saraceni, et etiam heretici* (*Disputed Questions de Trinitate*, q.1, a.2).
16 II, 16 (BAC, p. 214).
17 III, 7 (BAC, p. 234).
18 XX, 3 (BAC, p. 556).
19 XX, 6 (BAC, p. 558).
20 Beginning in 1378 the popes of Avignon (Clement VII, Benedict XIII, Alexander V, John XXIII) and those of Rome (Urban VI, Boniface IX, Innocent VII, Gregory XII) were dividing Christian Europe.
21 XXII, 1 (BAC, p. 606).
22 XXII, 2 (BAC, p. 606-607).
23 I, 2 (BAC, p. 178).
24 XXII, 2 (BAC, p. 606).
25 XXII, 3 (BAC, p. 608). In XXI, 23 the Thrones, "in whom God is said to sit," are mentioned after God the Father, then the Cherubim, and lastly the Seraphim; this does not reverse the Dionysian hierarchic order (as said in David Keck, *The Angelology of St. Bonaventure*, Ann Arbor: University of Michigan Press, 1990, p. 107, and echoed in Colt Anderson, *A Call to Piety*, p. 166-167); the Seraphim are still the highest of angels; they evoke the First Person residing in the Third. On Bonaventure's angelology, see Tavard, *Die Engel* (*Handbuch der Dogmengeschichte, Bd II, Fasz. 2B*, Freiburg: Herder, 1968, p. 66-70).
26 XXII, 6-7 (BAC, p. 608-610).

[27] *Si cupis elevari ad secundum et tertium coelum, sit tibi transitus per primum, id est cor tuum* (*De Perfectione vitae ad sorores*, ch. 1, n.6, in *Decem opuscula...*, 3rd edition, Quarachi, 1926, p. 256).

[28] XXII, 11 (BAC, p. 612); Bonaventure analyzed the three ways with great subtlety in his opusculum *De triplici via*.

[29] In former times they effectively watched the gates and stopped the "immodest, excommunicates, energumens, catechumens, and infidels," whereas, Bonaventure complains, "today, pig and dog enter" (XXII, 11: BAC, p.612); one may presume that the expression, "pig and dog," at this point as elsewhere, designates Jews and heretics.

[30] XXII, 13 (BAC, p. 614).

[31] XXII, 14 (BAC, p. 614).

[32] Bonaventure follows the theology of priesthood and episcopacy that was universal in the medieval Latin Church: There is no higher "character" imprinted in the soul than what is conveyed by the sacrament of orders as received by priests; this theology was abandoned by Vatican Council II (*Lumen gentium*, 21).

[33] XXII, 15 (BAC, p. 614-616).

[34] XXII, 20 (BAC, p. 618).

[35] XXII, 21 (BAC, p. 618).

[36] XXII, 22 (BAC, p.620).

[37] Delorme, *Visio IV, collatio III, n. 20-23* (p. 256-257).

[38] XXII, 23 (BAC, p. 620).

[39] The visibility is not of the material order, and therefore the Church is not visible,—as Cardinal Bellarmine (1542-1621) will write in his *Controversies*,—like the Kingdom of France and the Republic of Venice.

[40] XXII, 24 (BAC, p.620).

Chapter 8
The Contemplative Church

The perspective that links together the angelic hierarchy in its Dionysian model and the actual hierarchy of the Church shows the Church militant as an institution of the created world that is subject to the influence of the angelic choirs, which are themselves, from high to low, regressive images of the Holy Trinity. This deeper structure unveils the ultimate purpose and role of the Church on earth: to reach a harmony that must be interior and spiritual, and not only institutional. Each Christian soul is destined to a parallel transformation, that will be actualized by a gratuitous flow of divine grace.

*

That the Church exists in each believer implies an experience of contemplation that has been described by many of the Catholic mystics. The contemplative soul is molded by what it contemplates, and this may be symbolically represented by the sun, the moon, and the stars, or, in patristic language, the Monarchy (or, more simply said, God), the Church, and the soul itself. "Only that soul is suspended in contemplation that has the sun, the moon, and the stars in its firmament[1]." God is of course supreme. As the moon "has some darkness and is not simply full of light," so in the Church militant "the irradiation goes through images and enigmas." Although this is not empirically observable, the soul's deeper reality is that of the Jerusalem that comes down from heaven. The meaning of images will be clear when the moon is full, that is, at the "opening of the Scriptures; and the book will be opened, and the seven seals broken, which have not yet been opened[2]."

Contrary to Joachim's assurance that he had discovered the key to the Scriptures, the opening of the book is reserved for the eschaton, "when our Lion of the tribe of Juda will arise and open the book," which is at the same time the book of Scripture and the book of Life. The expectation of a contemplative Church does not mean that a new Church is to come, but that the soul can reach a new spiritual level: "The contemplative Church and the soul differ only in that the Church has collectively [*multipliciter*] what the soul has in itself: Any soul has a certain perfection in order to see the visions of God when it is raised and maintained in contemplation[3]."

The internal structure that makes the soul similar to Jerusalem on high features twelve stars that illumine the heavenly city. It was an axiom of medieval humanism, however, that a close similarity unites macrocosm and microcosm, the created universe and the human body. Because the body is a reduced copy of the cosmos and it is ruled by the soul, one may see the cosmos within the soul: "The soul is a great thing: in the soul the whole universe can be inscribed,[4]" or, in a more philosophical formulation, "The soul is a great thing, for 'somehow the soul is every potency'[5]." As with Jacob's ladder ascent is first, descent second. But since a hierarchy always ends at its highest point there must be a second ascent, a return. Starting in the natural creation, the ascent passes through action done under the impact of grace. It succeeds by grace alone, beyond all that nature and human action can do by themselves[6].

The contribution of nature lies in the areas of language and of thought, as one speaks (*nuntiatio*), decides (*dictatio*), and passes on to implementation (*ductio*), processes that Bonaventure compared to Angels, Archangels, and Principalities. Action with grace continues as the soul seeks God as its ultimate purpose (Powers), in a difficult search that needs assistance (Virtues) and support (Dominations). Taken beyond nature and beyond action, the soul becomes entirely passive under grace, when, "raised above itself, and having abandoned itself, it receives divine lights and reflects what is given to it from above[7]." The process includes reception, revelation, union, on the model of the Thrones, Cherubim, and Seraphim. It illustrates the fundamental capacities through which the soul is able to receive gifts (Seraphim), to preserve them (Cherubim), and in turn to give them back (Thrones)[8].

A fundamental desire for God—*charitas*—is inscribed in the human soul, where it inspires adoration and personal humility. Adoration passes through the three levels of outside (*extra nos*), inside (*intra nos*), and above (*supra nos*), that are crowned with glory when the soul becomes, like the Seraphim, "one Spirit with God[9]." The outside, *extra,* comprises all the things of nature. In the conclusion of *De reductione artium ad theologiam* Bonaventure had written: "The multiform wisdom of God... is hidden in every cognition and in every nature... It is even patent how wide is the way of enlightenment, and how in everything that is perceived or known, there God himself lies within[10]." If God truly resides in all things, how much more deeply and intimately does he not reside in all human souls? At this point, when it is truly one with God, the soul indeed is truly "the sun-clad Woman, with the moon under her feet, and on her head a crown of twelve stars, because she is filled with lights and never loses sight of the light[11]." The soul is fully equipped for the spiritual journey. It has the necessary tools to examine (like Angels), to choose (like Archangels), to act (like Principalities). It has interior virtues to control passions (like Powers), to overcome laziness and inertia (like Virtues), to desire the spiritual achievement in which it will become the Temple of God (like Dominations). It also has higher virtues to welcome God's doing (like Thrones), to look around and admire the actions of God and their divine Author (like Cherubim), so that it may finally be caught up in God as God's own beloved (like Seraphim). The soul is now able to focus without blinking as she travels from star to star[12].

*

Even though the symbolic universe of our medieval ancestors seems arbitrary today, it remains that all Christians are called to the contemplative enjoyment of God, partially in this life, "as in a glass, darkly" (1 Cor. 13, 13), and fully in the next. That the contemplative soul is itself the contemplative Church has been illustrated by the mystics who, from the time of Elijah and Merkabah mysticism, and at all periods of Christian history, have traveled and described their itinerary to God. In part because of Joachim, the spirituals of the thirteenth century liked to see this journey in the life of St. Francis. The Seraph became an appropriate symbol for the mystic ascent, and Francis a model of the highest Christian experience, because, in his seraphic vision of La Verna, on September 17, 1224, Francis took part in the dying of Christ, and saw "the truth of what He said on the Cross to the good thief, 'This day you will be with me in paradise'[13]." Gherardo da Borgo San Donnino, however, had gone much further when he identified Francis with the angel of Apocalypse 7, 2, the opener of the sixth and final age of the world.

As he narrated the life and miracles of Francis in the *Legenda major*, Bonaventure admitted a certain analogy between Francis and the angel of Apocalypse 7,2. At the opening of the sixth seal John of Patmos had seen four angels who were destined to wreak havoc on the earth. He had also seen a fifth angel, "who bore the sign of the Living God" (Apoc. 7, 2), and who was to restrain those four until the elect had been sealed with the mark of salvation:

> This herald, who was loved by Christ, imitable by us, and admirable to the world, was the Servant of God Francis, as we conclude with indubitable trust if we notice the summit of highest sanctity in him, by which, living among men, he imitated the angelic purity, which made him an example to the perfect disciples of Christ[14].

Not only did Francis adopt a penitential way of life. He was also marked with "the sign of resemblance with the Living God, Christ crucified, that was imprinted in his body not by virtue of nature or the artifice of art, but rather by the admirable power of the Spirit of the Living God[15]." The assertion that Francis was made to partake of angelic purity in his vision of a crucified Seraph may be seen as a gesture of peace toward the friends of John da Parma. Nevertheless, far from supporting the claim of the *Liber introductorius* regarding the Eternal Gospel, the vision of La Verna pointed in a totally different direction. Rather than unfold the literal sense of the biblical text it was an allegory. In fact Bonaventure did not allude to this in the *Legenda minor*, a simpler and shorter life of Francis in quasi-liturgical form, in which no less than nine "lessons" were devoted to the stigmata[16]. The hagiographic genre favored allegories, and it liked to dwell on miracles as signs of holiness. The evocation of Francis could easily emphasize the miracle of the stigmata. Despite Gherardo da Borgo San Donnino, however, the Franciscans were not the 144000 elect of the Apocalypse: Neither the Friars minor nor the Friars preachers belong to the highest Order, in which Francis stands alone[17].

The symbolism of numbers, inherited from Augustine, remained important to the medieval mind, especially when the blueprints of Gothic churches placed the diverse parts of a building in proportional relations centered on a golden number. In this architectonic context the biblical use of numbers was striking enough to call for prolongations and speculations. Is it truly significant, however, that 12 multiplied by 12 (twelve insights 'in,' multiplied by twelve insights 'through') gives 144, which is the apocalyptic number of the Holy City, with ramparts of 144 cubits (Apoc. 21, 17) and 144000 inhabitants (7, 4 and 14, 1)? In the thirteenth century this meant that the Holy City is made of the souls that have risen to the contemplation of God. Such apocalyptic references also had a polemical edge: The highest level that can be reached in the ascent to God provides the most effective refutation of Joachim's eschatology and its Eternal Gospel. For since it presupposes the indwelling of the Three Persons in the soul, it cannot be reached without an interior manifestation of these divine Persons and the mediation of the Incarnate Word.

The angel of Apocalypse 7, 2 opens the sixth age of the Church, the time of the second advent: "There are six ages, the sixth itself having three periods and a time of rest[18]." The time of rest will truly be the age of contemplation, but be so different from what Joachim had announced that Bonaventure says: "The contemplative Church and the soul do not differ, except that the soul has in itself all that the Church has in a multitude." Not by its own capacity, however, does the soul in contemplation acquire the features of the Church. This can only be the fruit of grace:

> When the soul is raised by imparted vigor, splendor, and ardor, it venerates piously, contemplates clearly, tastes saintly, and through this it understands in its own mode the long eternity, the wide charity, the high power, the deep wisdom of the Principle near which it must abide[19].

Vigor, splendor, and ardor are aspects of divine grace that enable the soul to adore, contemplate, and taste, and so to grasp, the eternity, charity, power, and wisdom of God. What the soul contemplates is within itself. The soul becomes its own horizon, in which it worships a vigor, contemplates a beauty, tastes a holiness, that are no other than God's vigor, beauty, and holiness. An unspoken principle, at the same time utterly simple and profoundly paradoxical, is at work here: At this level of contemplation seeing and being are not two distinct activities, but only one. The soul's level of contemplation is the level of its being. The contemplative soul becomes what it sees, namely, Jerusalem in the three forms of the Heavenly City, in heaven, descending from heaven, and returning to heaven[20]. None of this is a personal achievement. It is the fruit of God's grace. By the same token the soul shares the Principle's eternity, charity, power, and wisdom, though evidently in its own imperfect mode.[21]

Such a soul sees something of the Trinity, and what it sees it in a sense becomes. It is the Heavenly City. It is four-sided, in that it sees how "the Principle causes all things by sublime power, governs all with deep wisdom, mends all with extended charity or benevolence, rewards all with long eternity[22]." The soul "understands the Sun itself according to substance, power, and operation, and sees all things in their reduction to the eternal Law." *Reductio*, a key term in Bonaventure's vocabulary, designates a theological method that looks at all things in light of the First Principle. It thus points to the very foundation of created reality, which exists in the material world to the extent that it is regulated by the eternal Law and resides in the eternal Mind. The Heavenly City that descends to earth is "the assumed Humanity" of the Son of God, "the living bread from heaven." All the dimensions of the Incarnation,—the birth, life, death, rising, ascending of Jesus, and his return as the Judge of all,—become present in contemplation. Finally, the "hierarchized" soul experiences and understands God's love as "unbreakable link, unrestricted gift, inextinguishable fire, incomprehensible consolation." Bonaventure goes on: "Then it sees the City of God, that is, itself, and it has four sides,[23]" namely, breadth, length, height, and depth. The breadth is predestination, "by which God always loves, and has always loved, and will always love the predestined with eternal charity[24]." The length is nothing less than all created things, with their adornment and organization according to "mode, species, and order." The height is a "seal of truth" that makes the soul "a closed garden, a sealed fountain." It is the fire of charity lit by the Incarnation, "the indissoluble chain"of the charity of Christ, "the unbreakable gift" of loving "all: God, and friends, and enemies, and foreigners, and neighbors." That love is the seal of truth was implied in a tradition that originated with Gregory the Great and had been underlined by St. Bernard and William of St.-Thierry: Love is itself a form of understanding and, in the mystical ascent, it reaches further than the intellect. The depth is the ultimate endowment of glory. For the delight is then so overwhelming that it can be neither understood nor explained, and it anticipates the glorification of "body and soul, that they might be absorbed and inebriated by the dew of heaven." There can be no distinction at this point between heaven, which is God's dwelling place, the Church, and the human soul. As the Delorme text concludes,

> Thus you will see how the soul is tropologically the Holy City Jerusalem, built in heaven, descending from heaven, ascending to heaven, allegorically the Church, anagogically the homeland, the supercelestial or celestial hierarchy[25].

The image of the City of God, with its four sides facing East, West, North, and South, and three gates on each side, is enriched by two other images, the sealing of the elect by the angel, and the twelve tribes of Israel, that were named after the twelve sons of Jacob. The significance of the names had been explained in St. Jerome's opusculum, *De nominibus hebraicis*[26]. In Apocalypse 7, 4-8, twelve thousand members from each tribe bear the seal of the City of God. This is not, however, a matter of blood kinship. The lineage is spiritual. It corresponds to mystery, *mysterium* in the original Greek sense of the term, which denotes at the same time a holy darkness and an opening of the mind toward understanding and perceiving the light.

Like the gates of the City the seals are grouped three by three. Along each side a seal or gate corresponds to one aspect of the type of perfection that is exemplified by the side where it is set:

> The soul has in itself the divine worship of God, divine union with God, a divine zeal for God, a divine sense of God, so that in the organization of the City worship is East, union is South, zeal is North, perception (*sensus*) of God is West[27].

Facing East, the traditional direction of liturgical worship and the orientation of churches in expectation of the Lord's return with the rising sun, Judah stands for faith, "the spiritual foundation on which the Church is founded[28]"; Ruben represents repentance and humility; and Gad self-control and purity of heart. Facing South, the side of "quiet, conciliation, darkness or entrance into the dark", Aser means the desire of beatitude, Nephthali universal love, and Manasse contempt for and oblivion of what is not worth remembering, all of which are conditions of union with God. Facing North and the cold Winter winds, Simeon represents compassion, Levi zeal, Issachar patience in tribulation. Facing West, Zabulon is steadfastness of purpose, Joseph, sagacity, Benjamin, the ecstatic taste of contemplation:

> Fourthly, on the occidental side is the perfect perception (*sensus*) of God, which places the human in a state of perfect contemplation. On this side Zabulon, Nephthali,and Benjamin are located. For the perfect perception of God has two associates. Hence the state (*status*) of contemplation must be in total quiet. Hence it has three conditions, namely, a peaceful state of the high mansion, an acute intuition (*contuitus*) of wise discernment, an ecstatic leap (*excessus*) of delightful consolation[29].

In Genesis 49, 27, the blessing of Jacob on this youngest of his sons called him a rapacious wolf: "Benjamin, a rapacious wolf, eats his prey in the morning and divides the spoils in the evening[30]." If this hardly evokes contemplation to the modern mind, the symbolism of the hunt is not unknown in mystical literature. In the sixteenth century John of the Cross used it in his poem, *Tras de un amoroso lance*[31].

In his own time Bonaventure could find the symbolism of Benjamin in the writings of Richard of St. Victor on the mystical life, *Benjamin major* and *Benjamin minor*[32]. Among the sons of Jacob Benjamin stands for perfect contemplation, while Zabulon and Nephthali, Benjamin's associates, designate the peace that is necessary to this high degree of the contemplation of God. There can be no doubt that Bonaventure used this symbolism as marking a point against Joachim. For it openly contradicted Joachim's interpretation of the youngest son of Jacob. In the *Concordia*, Rachel's bearing of Benjamin symbolized the imperfect Cistercian Order, that was unwittingly pregnant with the perfect Order of Fiore. As Mary conceived in the sixth month of Elizabeth's confinement, as Joseph was born in the sixth year of Rachel's marriage and Benjamin followed Joseph, likewise in the sixth age of the Church the Fiorensians followed the Cistercians, who gave birth to them without realizing it. An imperfectly spiritual Order, in which contemplation was hindered by action, carried the potency of the purely contemplative Order that would inaugurate the Church of the Last Days. A mixture of metaphors,—here, a confusion of pregnancies,—never bothered Joachim very much. The purely contemplative Order, the God-given model for the spiritual Church of the Holy Spirit, could only be the Order of San Giovanni in Fiore, and all the more so as, according to St. Jerome, the Hebraic word, Nazareth, means, in Latin, *flos*, "flower[33]." In this logic San Giovanni in Fiore must be the true Nazareth.

Seen by Bonaventure, however, the future order is neither, as Joachim expected, a monastic order yet to come, nor, as Gherardo claimed, the Order of St. Francis. It is the order of grace, that is open to all the faithful through the Holy Spirit. This order implies the fulfillment of the Law. And it holds the promise of lasting for ever since it anticipates the seventh age, the age of the eternal Kingdom. Indeed the traditional image of Benjamin, for whom Rachel died in childbirth, represents the fullness of grace that is experienced in the highest contemplation:

> Finally there is the ecstatic taste of sweet contemplation. From the tribe of Benjamin, he said, twelve thousand marked. Benjamin, son by the right hand, son of sorrow, in whose birth Rachel died, and nevertheless Benjamin, the Lord's most beloved, will remain all day as though in the nuptial chamber; and he signifies the ecstatic leap [*excessus*] of contemplation[34].

After Benjamin, "no more son is born to Jacob." As in John of the Cross's *Ascent of Mount Carmel*, the way peters out at the top of the mountain, which is reached only by the few, that is, by those who have passed through the eleven previous steps and been marked by all the previous seals. John of the Cross will write: "Here there is no longer any way because for the just man there is no law, he is a law unto himself[35].» One cannot go any further in the present life, except perhaps in the "rapture" that Bonaventure had no time to describe since his elevation to the cardinalate brought his *Lectures on the Six Days* to an untimely end.

Notes

1 The switch to this deeper reality takes place at XXII, 24, and the explanation fills the second half of this lecture (24-43) and the entire *Collatio* XXIII; the Delorme edition ends *Collatio* XXII (equivalently, *Visio* IV, *collatio* III) after n. 23, and it makes 24-42 the first part of *Visio* IV, *collatio IV,* which is the last lecture. As he indicated at the opening of his lectures, Bonaventure originally intended to study also prophecy and the rapture, a rare spiritual level that medieval exegetes understood St. Paul to have reached (2 Cor. 12, 3-4). That this part of the plan was not fulfilled was due to Bonaventure's sudden promotion, when, on 3 June 1273, Gregory X made him a cardinal and bishop of Albano, and ordered him to travel immediately to the papal residence in Orvieto. They journeyed together, it seems, to the Second Council of Lyon, which opened on 7 May 1274. Bonaventure died during the council, on 15 July 1274, the eve of the fifth session.

2 XX, 2 (BAC, p. 556).

3 XX, 15 (BAC, p. 566).

4 Delorme, *Visio* IV, *collatio* IV, 4; p. 265.

5 XXI, 4 (BAC, p. 582).

6 Delorme, *Collatio* IV, 1; reference is given to Aristotle, *De anima* III.

7 *Et ideo nos debemus attribuere industriae cum natura, industriae cum gratia, et gratiae super naturam et industriam* (XXII, 24: BAC, p. 620).

8 XXII, 27 (BAC, p. 622).

9 XXII, 28-31 (BAC, p.622-624).

10 *De Reductione artium ad theologiam,* n. 26: Emma Therese Healy, *Saint Bonaventure's De Reductione artium ad theologiam* (*Works of Saint Bonaventure,* vol. 1, St. Bonaventure, NY: Franciscan Institute, 1955, p. 40).

11 XXII, 31 (BAC, p. 624). Bonaventure names these twelve points of light: bodily natures, spiritual substances, intellectual sciences, moral virtues, instituted divine laws, infused graces, just judgments, incomprehensible mercies, merits, rewards, temporal succession, eternal reasons (XXII, 40: BAC, p. 632).

12 XXII, 39 (BAC, p. 630).

13 *Itinerarium* ch.7, 2.

14 *Hunc nuntium amabilem Christo, imitabilem nobis, et admirabilem mundo, servum Dei fuisse Franciscum, indubitabili fide colligimus, si culmen in eo eximiae sanctitatis advertimus, quo inter homines vivens imitator fuit puritatis angelicae, qua et positus est perfectis Christi sectatoribus in exemplum* (*Leg-*

enda S. Francisci, prologue, n.2, in *Seraphici Doctoris Sancti Bonaventurae Legendae Duae,* Quaracchi: Collegio S. Bonaventurae, 1898, p.3)

15 *...verum etiam irrefragabili veritatis testificatione confirmat signaculum similitudinis Dei viventis, Christi videlicet crucifixi, quod in corpore ipsius fuit impressum non per naturae virtutem vel ingenium artis, sed potius per admirandam potentiam Spiritus Dei vivi* (*Legenda major,* prologue, n.3, in *Legendae duae,* p.3).

16 *Legendae duae,* p.256-263.

17 In view of these deliberate differences between Bonaventure's view of Francis and the Joachimite line of thought, some modern authors are, like the popes of the thirteenth century, far too lenient toward Joachim, e.g. Joseph Ratzinger, *The God of Jesus Christ,* Chicago: Franciscan Herald Press, 1979, p. 98-100.

18 XXIII, 4 (BAC, p.638-640). "Three periods" is a correction made by the Quaracchi editors where the manuscripts have six. Marc Ozilou esteems the correction possible, but unlikely (*Les Six Jours...,* p.496, note 36). Three periods, however, not six, are itemized in the following sections, 5-13. In addition, in XVI, 29 Bonaventure said of the sixth period of the Old Testament: *In sexto tempore facta sunt tria: praeclaritas victoriae, praeclaritas doctrinae, praeclaritas vitae propheticae* ("In the sixth period three things happen, the splendor of victory, the splendor of doctrine, the splendor of prophetic life"); this tallies with the Quaracchi correction.

19 XXIII, 6 (BAC, p. 640).

20 XXIII, 5 (BAC, p. 640).

21 Delorme, *Visio IV, collatio IV,* 5-6, p.266. The Delorme version clarifies this. Instead of evoking "the Principle," it refers explicitly to the Holy Trinity as it says that eternity, charity, power, and wisdom are *in ipsa Trinitate,* "in the Trinity itself."

22 XXIII, 6 (BAC, p. 640).

23 XXIII, 9 (BAC, p. 642). Delorme, *Visio IV, collatio IV,* n.9 (p. 267): "Then it sees the four sides of the City of God, that is, of itself."

24 XXIII, 10 (BAC, p. 642-644).

25 Delorme, *Visio IV, collatio IV* (p. 267-268)

26 PL 23, 771-858.

27 Delorme, *Visio IV, collatio IV,* n.15 (p. 269).

28 XXIII, 16 (BAC, p. 646); the analogy is pursued in the rest of this *collatio.*

29 Delorme, *Visio IV, collatio IV,* n.27 (p. 258).

30 *Benjamin lupus rapax mane comedet praedam, et vespere dividit spolia.* Reading a somewhat different Latin version, *Benjamin, lupus rapax, mane rapiet, ad vesperum dividit spolia* (Sermo 279, 1; PL 38, 1275), Augustine understood it as meaning: "Benjamin, a rapacious wolf, captures in the morning and divides the spoils in the evening," and he had applied the formula to St. Paul. This is also echoed by Bonaventure: "In the mystery

of the gift of grace, Christ is shown as generous giver [*diffusor*, or, in Delorme, *donator*] in the Acts, when he gave the Holy Spirit, as pious giver, as in Paul, in whom the Acts of the Apostles had their consummation... for he [Paul] was Benjamin and a rapacious wolf, the last of the Apostles, through whom the future order was signified. He was shown as a prudent giver in the canonical epistles, as a wise giver in Paul's epistles" (XIV, 28: BAC, p. 446).

[31] On this poem see Tavard, *Poetry and Contemplation in St. John of the Cross*, Athens, OH: Ohio University Press, 1988, p. 168-173.

[32] Claire Kirchberger, *Richard of Saint-Victor. Selected Writings on Contemplation,* New York: Harper, no date.

[33] "Flower, or its buds, or purities, or separate, or protected" (PL 23, 842); anyone of these meanings would fit Joachim's hopes for his monastery; Wessley, *Joachim...,* p. 37-38; 108.

[34] XXIII, 30 (BAC, p. 654).

[35] Kieran Kavanaugh and Otilio Rodriguez, *The Collected Works of St. John of the Cross,* Washington: ICS Publications, 1991, p. 111.

Epilogue

The story that the preceding pages have told fits in the horizon of the Augustinian tradition. This was never a clear-cut system. The most Augustinian among the medieval theologians felt quite free to depart from some of the positions of Augustine and also, as Joachim himself did, from the interpretations of one of his most revered distant disciples, Peter Lombard. In the great doctors of scholasticism it was possible to absorb elements of Aristotelian metaphysics without thereby renouncing traditional theology. The works of the Doctor of Hippo and of Dionysius enshrined the Christian dogmas in an intellectual framework of largely neo-Platonic origin, even though these sources were known, as often they must have been, through partial collections of sentences. To this basic framework scientific elements borrowed from grammarians and rhetoricians, and philosophical elements derived from the logic and the ethics of Aristotle had been added through the years. The development of the medieval tradition before the thirteenth century had prepared the minds for further adaptations, for which the progressive discovery of Aristotelian metaphysics, understood through Avicennian and Averroist commentaries, provided ample material.

The most important of the underlying concepts was that of «exemplarism,» namely, the assumption that the similarities of all creatures are best explained by reference to a common model, which ultimately is God, the Creator. Since this relation to God belongs in the very essence of creatures it is the task of the human creatures, endowed with intellect and will, to become more like God in their life, by imitating Christ and listening to the inspirations of the Spirit. The story of Joachim is inevitably tied up with the question: Can this likeness to God include participation in the divine knowledge of the future, and especially of the eschatological future, that must coincide with the ultimate transformation of the earthly Church into the heavenly Church?

Joachim obviously thought so, at least in his own case. He thought that this belief came from experience, and it was powerful enough for him to challenge what had hitherto been the general view of a slow progress of the Church toward a human destiny that cannot be fully depicted because it is in the hands of God. As he presented a vision that totally upset the Church's self-understanding, Joachim paradoxically professed full adherence to the traditions and decisions of *ecclesia romana*.

*

Joachim and his posthumous adversaries had divergent visions of the Church and of what may be called ecclesial esthetics. Although this is not ordinarily considered in relation to the structure of faith, a dimension of creativity is inseparable from a living faith. In his many writings on theological esthetics Hans Urs von Balthasar related it to the sense of the glory of God. In my own study of the great Mexican poet, Sor Juana (1648-1695), I traced her theology of beauty to the "mythopoetic function of faith[1].» All theologians agree that there are two essential dimensions of faith, namely belief and trust. In the split that occurred in Christendom in the sixteenth century the Protestant side gave the dominant, though by no means exclusive importance to trust, and the Catholics to belief. The third dimension of faith derives from the impulse to make belief and trust instruments for building new visions of the world, better, more satisfying, and more beautiful than the ambiguous spectacle of mixed good and evil that strikes any person who looks at the world with wide-opened eyes. Here lies the origin of Christian imagination, as it has been given expression in preaching, hermeneutics, hymnology, poetry, art, architecture, in the literature of utopias, in the dreams of an ideal world that many simple believers entertain and on which, at their best moments, they pattern their life. In the Oriental Churches this dimension of faith has been channeled by tradition toward an iconography guided by an elaborate theology of icons. In the Western Churches it has generally been left to the private initiatives of those who are gifted enough to explore it at various levels of imagination and creativity.

It is, let me suggest as the central conclusion of the present work, in relation to this mythopoetic dimension of faith that Joachim should be understood. At the level of explicit belief Joachim was undoubtedly, as Honorius III affirmed and Alexander IV implicitly agreed, a good Catholic. What happened when his imagination led him into myth-making was and remains, precisely, the question. The response, in my view, is clear: His imagination distorted faith by adding to trust and belief an expectation that was not grounded in the revelation of Christ, was incompatible with the traditional belief in the Holy Trinity, and effectively brought a fatal imbalance to the hope in God's future that always accompanies belief. The myth that Joachim invented implicitly contradicted belief and explicitly distorted trust. One may well agree with Thomas Aquinas that Joachim was not smart enough to notice the full impact of what he was doing; but if this may be a personal excuse it neither justifies his prophecy of the coming of the Eternal Gospel, nor excuses those who in later ages have put their trust in some form of spiritual utopia. The question is in fact broader than Joachim's own case: What happens to the integrity of faith when the imagination, initially prompted by trust and belief, goes wild, and escapes the limits that belief and trust should spontaneously assign to myth-making?

*

When Joachim sought for the beauty of the Church, he found it depicted in the Apocalypse and in what the abbot understood the Apocalypse to say. In the helleno-roman civilization that the Middle Ages had inherited from the Roman Empire, beauty was primarily associated with Greek sculpture and secondarily with Greek and Latin oratory and poetry. Acting as poles of attraction of the esthetic sense, the former focused attention on the human body, male and female, taken as the epitome of temporal beauty, and the latter on the use of grammar and words in human discourse. In either case beauty was ephemeral, destined, like bodies, to deteriorate with age and pass away, or, like language, to vanish once spoken, little by little to fade from living memory, and, when written, to deteriorate also along with its material support.

In Christian theology beauty was essentially related to a vision of the Church, both the Church of the Old Testament and that of the New, as the esthetic work of God at its fullest. It is a priori evident that any search for beauty in the context of faith implies the preliminary conviction that the Creator is not only Supreme Being and Supreme Goodness, but also Supreme Beauty. Even so, there was little discussion among the scholastics of beauty as the fourth transcendental, being, goodness, and oneness being the first three. As to the biblical interest in beauty, it is present as a backdrop to the poems of the Old Testament, in the Psalms, and in the Song of Songs. Featured in the Song of Songs as an object of contemplation, it is extolled as a quality of the human body that is perceived in the reciprocity of sexual love. Commentaries on the spiritual symbolism of the Song's glittering images were not rare in monastic literature, especially among Cistercians. St. Bernard composed eighty-five sermons on the Song of Songs, and his friend William of St.-Thierry wrote a commentary on it.

Neither Thomas nor Bonaventure commented on the Song. The scholastics indeed upheld the principle that the spiritual senses of Scripture should not stifle attention to the literal sense. In both the classical heritage and the biblical tradition visible beauty was primarily associated with the nude body. And nakedness was much more acceptable in medieval culture than it later became. Like the rabbis, who considered the *Shir hashirim* unfit reading for the young, the scholastics hesitated before the obviously erotic dimension of the Song in its letter. It is all the more remarkable that some of Bonaventure's writings treated beauty as a major category of Christian contemplation in the illuminative way. *De triplici via* located *speciositas* at the third degree of contemplation, on the way that leads to perceiving "the splendor of Truth" (*splendor veritatis):*

> Thirdly, consider how great is the one who suffers [in the Passion], go to him through admiration, and see how immense he is in power, beauty (*speciositas*), felicity, eternity. Admire therefore how immense power is annihilated, beauty discolored, felicity threatened, eternity dying[2].

In a poem that is at the heart of *Lignum vitae*, the last but one appellation of Jesus is *fontalis radius*, "fontal ray," in the sense of "beam radiating from the Source[3]." The commentary explains it in terms of clarity, light, and splendor. Christ Jesus is "a super-essential ray" that makes all things new, "a true emanation of the clarity of the virtue of almighty God," the "font of life and light." The devout soul is exhorted to exclaim:

> O inaccessible beauty of Most High God, pure clarity of eternal light, life vivifying all life, light (*lux*) illumining all light (*lumen),* and keeping in perpetual splendor the myriads of lights that flash before the throne of Divinity since the very first dawn!

The beauty of Christ entails the beauty of faith and the beauty of the Church. Despite their polemical edge, this beauty lay at the heart of the Lectures on the Six Days, rather than the errors, sources of ugliness, that threatened it. The Word of God, centered on Jesus Christ as the sevenfold Mediator of metaphysics, physics, mathematics, dialectics, ethics, law, and theology (Lecture I), leads the reader, through the gate of Wisdom, to an ecstatic admiration of its four qualities as uniform, multiform, omniform, and nulliform Wisdom (II), by way of the contemplative dimension of the gift of intellect. This gift provides a triple key of contemplation, an understanding of the Word Uncreated, Incarnate, and Inspired (III). Through this gift the reader discovers the truth that can be reached by natural knowledge (IV-VII), by faith (VIII-XII), by the perusal of Scripture (XIII-XIX), and by contemplation (XX-XXIII). A reference to architecture is explicit in the last lecture: "There are therefore three Eastern doors, three Southern doors, three Northern doors, three Western doors[4]." A porch having three doors, as in Gothic architecture, there are four porches, each of which leads to God as the ultimate Truth, the Truth that preexists, sustains creation, recreates, and brings to consummation.

In the actual structure of a church building, the Eastern porch is virtual. Clergy and people turn to the orient in prayer and expectation, and their prayer is carried up, beyond the walls, towards the coming Christ of the Second Advent. The three other porches are actual gates. The two that represent creation and recreation,—South and North,—open on the transept, where the creature and divine grace meet at the Cross of Jesus. The Western porch, that is mostly used to enter and exit from a church-building, is frequently decorated, in cathedrals and larger churches, with sculptures of the Last Judgment.

It introduces to the consummation of human life, when the faithful come face to face with their God.

In this way the four porches mark out a quadrilateral, the center of which is occupied by the Savior, crucified and risen. Thus already the natural world, with the four directions of East, West, North, and South, reveals a Christ-centered coherence. The human creatures experience the truth of created entities (*rerum*), of language (*vocum*), and of mores (*morum*), when the mind is illumined by the eternal light of the divine Exemplar. In such a setting neither is faith alien to nature, nor is nature abandoned to itself. The heart of the Church is nothing else than the beauty of faith, *speciositas fidei*, *formositas*, which itself reflects God's beauty, since created beauty presupposes an Eternal Model. Reciprocally, faith so perceives the Church's elegance and luminosity that the occasional darkness of its history fades and is absorbed in true enlightenment, when the soul is illumined by the divine Word.

As a work of God, the Church is intimately related to the divine works that have preceded it, the angelic world and the material universe. The pattern is of a descending scale of resemblance. The prime analogue being the Trinity of divine Persons, closest to it are the angels, and the cosmos is further down the scale, along with, perhaps, other universes that remain invisible to human eyes. Within their own cosmos, human beings are themselves personally modeled on the Trinity. And since they are at the same time material and spiritual, a series of progressive likenesses of the Three Persons abides in them. By nature they are, on an ascending scale, shadows (*umbra*), vestiges (*vestigium*), and images (*imago*) of the Three Persons. By grace they can also be similitudes (*similitudo*).

The basic conception derives from the Syrian monk known as Dionysius the Areopagite, active in the late fifth century, whose works found an enthusiastic audience in the West when they were translated in Latin, partly because he was often believed to have been divinely inspired and to have been the first bishop of Paris. The scholastics had no cause to doubt the identity of this author as the disciple of St. Paul who had been converted in Athens (Acts 17, 34). The exact authorship of his works, in any case, has little bearing on the depth and extent of his influence.

Being of this world without belonging to it, the Church bears the mark of the Trinity at the two levels of the material and the spiritual. It is patterned on the angelic hierarchies described by Dionysius. History, which has largely determined the shape of the Church and its institutions, notably in regard to ministerial offices and functions, has not erased, although it has certainly dimmed, the analogy that Dionysius perceived between the human Church and the angelic community. Unlike Thomas Aquinas, who thought that angels are so profoundly different from one another that each one constitutes a solipsist genus, Bonaventure held that, like humans, they constitute one species, the differences among them coming from the choir of which each is a member.

Something happened to this vision of the Church when, in the fifteenth century, the humanist Lorenzo Valla (c.1407-1457) disproved the Dionysian authorship of the works attributed to the Areopagite, on the basis of their style and contents. Following this, the Reformers never admitted their authority, and Catholic theologians became much less enthusiastic about these writings than the scholastics had been. Dionysius has nevertheless remained a favorite author in the mystical tradition of spirituality. In spite of what seems to be a mild form of Monophysitism, he is still held in high regard in the Orthodox Church. By and large, however, Dionysius is no longer a live source of thinking and speculation in Catholic theology. The dearth of biblical material regarding the nature of angels as creatures distinct from humanity is such that the attention paid to the metaphysics of angelology by the great doctors of the thirteenth century is disconcerting to many today. Not a few scholars indeed would relegate angels to a mythical world with symbolic import, but no solid reality.

It was Calvin's judgment that the term, hierarchy, which also comes from Dionysius, is unfortunate, if not as regards angels,—of them we really know very little,—at least as defining teaching authority and liturgical presidency in the People of God. The term, Calvin rightly noted, "is not used in Scripture, for the Holy Spirit wanted to avoid that, in the matter of church government, one should imagine some principality or domination[5]." It was also, he remarked, unknown to the ancients. In the Catholic Church, however, a triumphalism of authority, as the Reformer feared, became a feature of the counterreformation.

It lasted as late as the pontificate of Pius XII. And it would not be hard to find traces of it in more recent Catholic literature, including magisterial documents.

In spite of this, some valid theological notation remains attached to the heavenly hierarchies. In the first place, the Three divine Persons are the necessary and only model of all that God creates. In the second place, the external works of God, *ad extra,* are indeed one in their diversity. The unity of nature has in fact become a hot topic in contemporary sciences. And there must be relationships, though mostly unperceived or unimagined, between and among all the divine works, visible and invisible, material and spiritual, earthly and heavenly. In a famous sonnet the poet Charles Baudelaire (1821-1867) celebrated such "correspondences" at the level of nature:

> *La Nature est un temple où de vivants piliers*
> *Laissent parfois sortir de confuses paroles.*
> *L'homme y passe à travers des forêts de symboles*
> *Qui l'observent avec des regards familiers*[6]*...*
> (Nature is a temple in which living pillars
> At times let obscure words escape.
> Man goes through them as through a forest of symbols
> That observe him with their familiar looks...)

On the basis of these correspondences Baudelaire posed the question of a "reversibility," an exchange, between the angelic and the human world:

> *Ange plein de gaieté, connaissez-vous l'angoisse...?*
> *Mais de toi je n'implore, ange, que tes prières,*
> *Ange plein de bonheur, de joie et de lumières!*
> (Angel full of gaiety, do you know anxiety...?
> Of you, angel, I beg only your prayers,
> Angel full of beauty, full of joy and of lights!)

Following the symbolist poetry, the linguistic analysis of symbols and language that developed in the second half of the twentieth century reopened the way to a search for invisible relationships, spiritual as well as ecological, among all creaturely beings.

*

Much of what Joachim wrote remained dormant after the failure of his prophecies to come true. In his studies on the abbot Henri de Lubac showed that Joachim's major orientations, if not the details of his views, never formally condemned by more than a provincial synod, resurfaced time and time again in the following centuries in the secular garb of utopian movements. As such they have not ceased to influence recent culture in the West[7]. It was a Joachim *redivivus*, disguised and distorted, who promised "singing to-morrows" to the workers of the world. At the opposite of the political spectrum, another utopian sick imagination promised a triumphal millennium to the Third Reich and its chosen race, and, in its effort to achieve it, brought death to millions of people. In the process, Adolf Hitler attempted to destroy the very basis of religious utopias that conflicted with his own hopes and ambitions. He was well aware of the distant origins of such utopias in the messianic expectations of traditional Judaism.

There have been other sequels of Joachimism in the horizon of Christianity. Traces of the Joachimite expectation, transformed by other times and cultures, have not only marked many a religious movement, and have also inspired decisions at the highest levels of Church that rested on false expectations, a utopian vision of the future. Pius V in 1570 excommunicated Queen Elizabeth in the mistaken trust that the English people, released by him of their natural allegiance to their Sovereign, would rise up and throw her out. The nineteenth century, shaken by the French Revolution, was rich in both secular and religious utopias, even in ecclesiastical circles, centered on, and at times encouraged or initiated by, the bishops of Rome. Several popes attempted to do with the utopias inspired by the French Revolution what Boniface had done with greater success when he opened the first Jubilee year in 1300, and oriented eschatological hopes, still more or less reminiscent of Joachim, toward reconciliation here and now through penance and indulgences, as the end of a century evoked an image of the end of times. Since the first pontifical "No!" in the eighteenth century (Pius VI, pope 1775-1799) was insufficient to stem the revolutionary tide, others followed, until Pius X (pope, 1903-1914), in the encyclical *Pascendi*, identified Modernism as "the sum total of all heresies," and tried to expel it from the Church by imposing the anti-modernist oath on the clergy[8]. In his reactionary fervor Pope Pius did not notice that he was himself pursuing a dream of purity that might be proper in an age of Latter-Day Saints, the very dream that his predecessors in the thirteenth century had not wished to outlaw, even when they fought its interpretation by the Spirituals. Nor did the popes of the nineteenth century realize that their fighting stance, however spiritual it was, fed the revolutionary illusion that violence can bring the millennium forward. There remained of course a major practical difference. Revolutionary violence was centered on the guillotine. Pontifical violence remained essentially verbal, though it could on occasion become more than verbal, as in the notorious kidnapping by the police of the Papal States of the six-year old Jewish boy, Edgar Mortara (1852-1940), in Bologna, in 1858. The boy had been baptized in secret. And to the pope's mind his unconscious right to a Christian education neutralized the demand of the natural law that he be educated by his parents. That Mortara was reconciled with his own history and became an Augustinian priest does not remove the opprobrium of Pius IX's action.

In post-revolutionary France, the dream of a new age was fueled by reaction to the memory of the Terror. Among many symptoms of utopian hopes, the *survivantiste* movement, that was inspired by a visionary peasant, Thomas Martin, and manipulated by several impostors, expected the quasi-miraculous reappearance of "Louis XVII," the young son of the martyred king Louis XVI, who was officially declared to have died on 8 June 1795 in the prisons of the Revolution[9]. With him as restored king, if he could be found, the government would recover its legitimacy, that is, its right to govern and the purity of its laws. The main claimant, Charles Naundorff (d. 1845), had the support of the "prophet" Eugène Vintras (1807-1875), who also announced the end of the Second Reign, that of Christ, and the imminent coming of the Third Reign, the Reign of the Paraclete. With Vintras and his followers the mythopoetic dimension of faith had gone mad.

Some of the numerous "apparitions of the Virgin" that were chronicled in France through the nineteenth century were not unrelated to the hope of a spiritual rebirth after the turmoil of the Revolution[10]. At the same period, and also in reaction to the Revolution, the Savoyan diplomat Joseph de Maistre (1753-1821) thought he read the signs of a new religious event that should unite the past and the future, tradition and prophecy. This was, as de Lubac put it, "still the great ecumenical dream in the pure Joachimite tradition, but joined to the most narrow 'catholicism'[11]." This prophetic concern was at the center of his posthumous publication, *Les Soirées de Saint-Pétersbourg* (1821). It was somehow in keeping with de Maistre's double loyalty, to the Christian faith in the Catholic Church and to the Masonic Lodge of Sincerity, that was active in Chambéry, the main city of the duchy of Savoia on the French side of the Alps.

Some twenty years later, the Polish poet Adam Mickiewicz[12] (1798-1855), exiled in Paris since 1832, reflected on his native land in a course he gave at the *Collège de France* on the topic, "the Official Church and Messianism" (*l'Eglise officielle et le messianisme*). Echoing the views of a would-be prophet who was somewhat deranged, Andrew Towianski (1799-1878), Mickiewicz gave a messianic scope to the sufferings of the Polish people under Russian and German occupation, a perspective to which he gave a more literary form in plays and other writings in Polish. While he always remained perfectly orthodox and faithful to the traditional Catholicism of Poland, he expected these sufferings to serve as a spark and model for a future age of peace and reconciliation.

While these hopes were nurtured among Polish exiles in Western Europe, the slavophile movement in Russia considered that the most thoroughly Christian people, in the tenor of its fundamental human experience no less than in its formal doctrines and liturgies, was no other than the Russian people[13]. Led by Alexei Khomiakov (1804-1860) and his son Dmitri (1841-1918), the movement gave a Russian Orthodox twist to a religious utopia that was germane to, and rival with, that of the Polish exiles. The dream of a future theocracy anchored in Russian culture was echoed in the novels of Fedor Dostoïevsky (1821-1881), whose Prince Muichkine, "the idiot," embodies the mind of the Russian peasantry together with the highest spiritual perfection.

*

Some of Joachim's ideas are still flowing like an underground stream in the Catholic Church. In 1989 and 1990 I received a few letters from a French lady, the late Denise Aimé-Azam, who contacted me after reading my book, *La Vision de la Trinité*[14]. She was in the process of collecting citations on the Trinity from biblical and Christian literature, which she hoped would be published, even posthumously, for she was herself in the late 80's. A cultured and very religious person, a convert from Judaism, who frequented the Benedictine abbey of En Calcat, she was a close friend of the mother of Simone Weil, and an admiring reader of Simone Weil's writings. She was by no means gullible or deluded. She, however, intensely felt what she called "an obsession with the Trinitarian relation." She looked for traces of this relation in the world where we live, and for texts in which Christian believers over the centuries have formulated their impressions of the Trinity. She thought that she could discern anticipations of the time of the Spirit in some trends of modern literature and in the charismatic movement. On November 5, 1983, she wrote:

> This obsession with the Trinitarian relation persuades me that, after the chaotic period that we are already living, the world will enter, with the twenty-first century, in a third Christian era: after that of the Father (Old Testament) and that of the Son (New Testament), that of the Spirit[15]...

Those who have read Joachim may easily hear between these lines an unconscious echo of what had been Joachim's passion: the preparation of the Church for the expected time of the Spirit that will bring about its spiritual transformation. Unlike Joachim, however, Denise Aimé-Azam did not focus her hopes on this third age, but on what she rightly perceived to be at the heart of Christian theology: "this idea of the theology of Relation, anchored in the Trinity, subsistent relation, and the basis of our faith[16].»

*

In 1974 in Cracow Carol Woytila wrote a poem that contains these lines:

> The tree of the knowledge of good and evil grew on the riverbanks of our land. Together with us it grew over the centuries; it grew into the Church through the roots of our conscience...
>
> This the liturgy of history. Vigil is the word of the Lord and the word of the People, which we continually receive anew. The hours pass into the psalms of ceaseless conversion: we move toward participation in the Eucharist of the worlds[17] ...

Composed as they were in a context of persecution, these verses transmit a faint echo of the vision of Adam Mickiewicz, the intellectual and spiritual mentor of modern Poland. Undoubtedly the sufferings of the People of God are not lost in the inter-galactic vacuum of a boundless universe. The faith knows their ultimate meaning to be in the believers' union with and participation in the suffering Christ, of whom the Gospel of Luke says, *Factus in agonia prolixius orabat* (Luke 22, 44), a verse that is unduly psychologized in some modern translations: «In his anguish he prayed more earnestly» (NRSV[18]). *Agonia,* at this point, does not only designate the subjective fear of a person who, like so many of our contemporaries, is facing the perspective of torture and death. It also describes the context in which Jesus lived, not just his last hours on earth, but all his life, the context of human life.

Catastrophes, natural disasters, wars plunge innocent people, who can only wait passively for whatever will happen, into a state of agony in which prayer, whether or not they believe that they are listened to by a transcendent Being, is the only possible recourse. It does happen, however, that certain conditions of collective suffering revive and nurture such hopes for recovery and renewal as seem to converge with the expectations which, in other troubled times, yet totally different circumstances, were formulated by the Calabrian abbot. As they have recurred time after time in the history of the Church, similar conditions have, over the centuries, painted a halo of legitimacy around the vaticinations of the false prophet of the twelfth-thirteenth century. And thus the perspective that Joachim had opened, erroneous as it was, and soon proved to be false, came to function as an avenue for the hope of the desperate. The crisis that Joachim opened, and that the popes of the thirteenth century left, in spite of their theologians, unresolved, nurtured long-lasting and far-reaching underground roots, that have in turn fed numerous shoots.

It is profoundly ironical that the implications of Joachim's peculiar method of biblical reading, the strange novelty of the eschatological perspectives he opened, and the dangerous orientations of his Trinitarian theology remained so long tolerated by the providential guardians of Catholic orthodoxy that they are now scarcely noticed.

Notes

1 *Juana Inés de la Cruz and the Theology of Beauty*, University of Notre Dame Press, 1991, p. 208-217.

2 *De triplici via* §3, n.3 (*Obras...*, vol. 4, p. 146).

3 *Lignum vitae* n. 47 (*Obras...*, vol. 2, p. 350).

4 *In Hexaëmeron* XXIII, n. 15 (*Obras...*, vol. 3, p. 646).

5 *Institutio christianae religionis*, 1558, IV, ch. 4, n.4.

6 *Les Fleurs du Mal* (originally published in 1857), poem n. 4; next quotation, poem n. 44.

7 This is precisely the topic of Henri de Lubac, *Postérité...*

8 Motu proprio *Sacrorum antistites* (1 September 1910): text in DS 3537-3550.

9 In recent years DNA analysis has established that the son of Louis XVI effectively died in the prisons of the Revolution.

10 *La Vierge Marie en France aux XVIIIe et XIXe siècles,* Paris: Le Cerf, 1998.

11 Henri de Lubac, *Postérité...*, vol. I, p. 299.

12 Mickiewicz is presented at length in de Lubac, *Postérité...*, II, p. 236-282.

13 Albert Gratieux, *A. S. Khomiakov et le mouvement slavophile*, 2 vol., Paris: Le Cerf, 1939; *Le mouvement slavophile à la veille de la Révolution. Dmitri A. Khomiakov*, Paris: Le Cerf, 1953.

14 *La Vision de la Trinité*, Paris: Le Cerf, 1989; English version: *The Vision of the Trinity*, Washington: University Press of America, 1981.

15 First letter addressed to the author, unpublished.

16 Text dated, 10 August 1990, included in a letter of 17 October 1990. Similar texts abound in the booklet she eventually published: *De la Relation. Florilège,* Abbaye d'En Calcat, 1995.

17 *The Place Within. The Poetry of Pope John Paul II*, translated by Jerzy Peterkiewicz, New York: Random House, 1994, p.148-149.

18 Compare with Ronald Knox's awkward but more objective translation: "And now he was in an agony, and prayed still more earnestly."

A Short Bibliography

(Besides the texts of Joachim I list a few authors who have provided me with ideas or information; the authors are not responsible for what I have written. Other references are given in the endnotes. The translations of Joachim are my own.)

Texts of Joachim

Tractatus super Quatuor Evangelia, Rome: Tipografia del Senato, 1930 (presented by E. Buonaiuti)

Liber de Concordia Novi ac Veteris Testamenti, Philadelphia: American Philosophical Society, 1983 (introduction and commentary by E. Randolph Daniel)

Liber introductorius in Apocalypsim, Frankfurt: Minerva, 1964

Expositio in Apocalypsim, Frankfurt: Minerva, 1964

Psalterium Decem Chordarum, Frankfurt: Minerva, 1965

Enchiridion super Apocalypsim, Toronto: Pontifical Institute of Medieval Studies, 1986

Translations

Works of Bonaventure, 6 vol., Bonaventure, NY, Franciscan Institute, 1945-1949.

José De Vinck, *The Works of Bonaventure*, 5 vol., Paterson: St. Anthony Guild Press, 1960-1970.

Marc Ozilou, tr., *Les Six Jours de la Création*, Paris: Desclée/Cerf, 1991; *Les Dix Commandements*, Paris: Desclée/Cerf, 1992. (These French translations have excellent introductions and footnotes)

Studies

Bernard McGinn, *The Calabrian Abbot: Joachim of Fiore in the History of Western Thought*, New York: Macmillan, 1985; *The Encyclopedia of Apocalypticism*, New York: Continuum, 1998; *Visions of the End: Apocalyptic Traditions in the Middle Ages*, New York: Columbia University Press, 1998

Marjorie Reeves, *The Influence of Prophecy in the Later Middle Ages*, Oxford: Clarendon Press, 1969; *Joachim of Fiore and the Prophetic Future*, London: SPCK, 1976

Marjorie Reeves and Beatrice Hirsch-Reich, *The Figurae of Joachim of Fiore*, Oxford: Clarendon Press, 1972

Henri de Lubac, *Medieval Exegesis,* 2 vol., Grand Rapids: Eerdmans, 1998-2000; *La Postérité spirituelle de Joachim de Flore*, 2 vol., Paris: Lethielleux, 1979-1981

Stephen E. Wessley, *Joachim of Fiore and Monastic Reform*, New York: Lang, 1990

Delno C. West, ed., *Joachim of Fiore in Christian Thought. Essays on the Influence of the Calabrian Prophet*, 2 vol., New York: Burt Franklin, 1975

Delno C. West and Sandra Zimdars-Swartz, *Joachim of Fiore. A Study in Spiritual Perception and History,* Bloomington: Indiana University Press, 1983

Marie-Dominique Chenu, *Toward Understanding St. Thomas,* Chicago: Regnery, 1964; *Aquinas and his Role in Theology*, Collegeville: Liturgical Press, 2002

George H. Tavard, *Transiency and Permanence. The Nature of Theology according to St. Bonaventure*, St. Bonaventure: Franciscan Institute, 1954

Guy Bougerol, *Introduction to the Works of Bonaventure*, Paterson: St. Anthony Guild Press, 1964

Josef Ratzinger, *The Theology of History in St. Bonaventure*, Chicago: Franciscan Herald Press, 1971

Zachary Hayes, *The Hidden Center. Spirituality and Speculative Christology in St. Bonaventure,* New York: Paulist Press, 1981

Charles Carpenter, *Theology as the Road to Holiness in St. Bonaventure*, Mahwah, NJ: Paulist Press, 1999

C. Colt Anderson, *A Call to Piety: Saint Bonaventure's Collations on the Six Days*, Quincy: Franciscan Press, 2002

Index